WA...

THIS BOOK W... E!

CW00971759

Today there is a booming discontent industry, consisting of entrepreneurs who cash in on your misery by selling you products that describe and decry it. Thus the exchange economy finds a place even for its enemies: perpetuating both industry and discontent as we struggle to fight them, we keep the wheels turning by selling more merchandise. And as in every other aspect of your lives, your real desires to make something happen are channeled into consuming—and your own abilities and potential are displaced, projected onto the "revolutionary" items you purchase.

This book could be a part of that process. While we hope we are using our product to "sell" revolution, it might be that we are just using "revolution" to *sell* our product.* The best of intentions can't protect us from this risk. But we've undertaken this project because we felt that, in addition to our other, less explicitly compromised activities, it might be worth giving the old experiment one more try: to see if a commodity can be created that *gives* more than it takes away.

For this book to have even the smallest chance of succeeding in that tall order, you can't approach it passively, you can't expect it to do the work. You have to regard it as a *tool,* nothing more. This book will not save your life; *that,* my friend, is up to *you.*

OK, that said, HERE WE GO!!!

*After all, in this society, if something isn't for sale, it might as well not exist—and it's almost impossible to think of anything to do with something of value besides market it.

Think about your direct bodily experience of life. No one can lie to you about that.

How many hours a day do you spend in front of a television screen? A computer screen? Behind an automobile windscreen? All three screens combined?

What are you being screened from?

How much of your life comes at you through a screen, vicariously? (Is watching things as exciting as *doing* things? Do you have enough time to *do* all the things that you want to? Do you have enough energy to?)

And how many hours a day do you sleep? How are you affected by standardized time, designed solely to synchronize your movements with those of millions of other people? How long do you ever go without knowing what time it is? Who or what controls your minutes and hours?

The minutes and hours that add up to your life?

Can you put a value on a beautiful day, when the birds are singing and people are walking around together? How many dollars an hour does it take to pay you to stay inside and sell things or file papers? What will you get later that could make up for this day of your life?

How are you affected by being in crowds, by being surrounded by anonymous masses? Do you find yourself blocking your emotional responses to other human beings?

And who prepares your meals? Do you ever eat by yourself? Do you ever eat standing up? How much do you know about what you eat and where it comes from? How much do you trust it?

What are we deprived of by labor-saving devices? By thought-saving devices? How are you affected by the requirements of efficiency, which place value on the product rather than the process, on the future rather than the present, the present moment that is getting shorter and shorter as we speed faster and faster into the future? What are we speeding towards?

Are we saving time? Saving it up for what?

How are you affected by being moved around in prescribed paths, in elevators, buses, subways, escalators, on highways and sidewalks? By moving, working, and living in two- and three-dimensional grids? How are you affected by being organized, immobilized, and scheduled... instead of wandering, roaming freely and spontaneously? Scavenging? (Shoplifting?)

How much freedom of movement do you have—freedom to move through space, to move as far as you want, in new and unexplored directions?

And how are you affected by waiting? Waiting in line, waiting in traffic, waiting to eat, waiting for the bus, waiting for
the bathroom—learning to punish and ignore your spontaneous urges?

How are you affected by holding back your desires?

By sexual repression, by the delay or denial of pleasure, starting
in childhood, along with the suppression of everything in you that
is spontaneous, everything that evidences your wild nature, your
membership in the animal kingdom?

Is pleasure dangerous? Could danger be joyous?

Do you ever need to see the sky? (Can you see stars in it any
more?) Do you ever need to see water, leaves, foliage, animals?
Glinting, glimmering, moving?

Is that why you have a pet, an aquarium, houseplants?
Or are television and video your glinting, glimmering, moving?

How much of your life comes at you through a screen, vicariously?

Do videotapes of yourself and your friends fascinate you,
as if you are somehow more real in image than in life?

If your life was made into a movie, would it be worth watching?
And how do you feel in situations of enforced passivity? How are
you affected by a non-stop assault of symbolic communication—
audio, visual, print, billboard, computer, video, radio, robotic
voices—as you wander through the forest of signs? What are
they urging upon you?

Do you ever need solitude, quiet, contemplation? Do you remember it? Thinking on your own, rather than reacting to stimuli? Is it
hard to look away?

Is looking away the very thing that is not permitted?

Where can you go to find silence and solitude? Not white noise, but
pure silence? Not loneliness, but gentle solitude?
How often have you stopped to ask yourself questions like these?
Do you find yourself committing acts of symbolic violence?
Do you ever feel lonely in a way that words cannot even express?

Do you ever feel ready to LOSE CONTROL?

*Additional copies of this book are available for $8ppd from
CrimethInc. HQ / 2695 Rangewood Dr. / Atlanta GA 30345,
or get current information at www.crimethinc.com*

Days of Love, Nights of War:

CRIMETHINK FOR BEGINNERS

your ticket out of this world

composed and published by
the Crimeth Inc. Workers' Collective

Warning: The word "revolution," which is used constantly throughout these pages with an unironic naiveté, may be amusing or off-putting to the modern reader, convinced as he is that effective resistance to the status quo is impossible and therefore not even worth considering. Gentle reader, we ask that you suspend your disbelief long enough to at least contemplate whether or not such a thing might be worthwhile if it <u>were</u> possible; and then that you suspend it further, long enough to recognize this disbelief for what it is—despair!

Table *of* Discontents

What is crimethink?

Today, everything that can't be bought, sold, or faked is crimethink.

Preface:
What is a "CrimethInc."?

A spectre is haunting the world today: the spectre of crimethink, and the underground front which heralds it. In every corporate washroom, on every street corner, under every roof from the ghettoes to the suburbs you can hear the whispers: "What is this CrimethInc.? Who are they? What do they want?"

These questions can be approached, if not answered. CrimethInc. is significant for what it is *not:* it is not a membership organization. It is not an elitist vanguard that purports to lead the masses out of darkness to salvation—experience has shown a thousand times that such parties are the social forces that *create* masses. And it is not a Movement, either: for such things only exist as a part of history, and as such are subject to its laws—gestation, ascendance, decline. As crimethink is a force that exists beneath the currents of history, outside the chain of events, CrimethInc. is the first stirrings of a revolt that will take us all *out* of history.

CrimethInc. is invincible because it is centerless, amoebic, invisible. Who is CrimethInc.? It could be anyone—the woman on the bus next to you could be one of us. Perhaps an autonomous CrimethInc. nucleus is at play in your town as you read this; perhaps *you* will form one when you're finished reading. Because CrimethInc. is an expression of longings that are in every heart, it could be just three travelers in an Italian hostel tonight and two hundred thousand independent cells in full blown insurrection next month.

As for what we want—you'd have to ask each of us, one by one, and hopefully you know better than to trust people when they answer *that* question.

It was said of one of our predecessors, a body of ex-artists and theorists active primarily in the 1960's, that their group was unique in that it represented a *stance* rather than an ideology ("not a position, but a proposition"). It would be tempting to say that CrimethInc. improves on their method in that it is founded on a shared desire, rather than a common critique; but this also misses the mark. CrimethInc. is a web of desires, all unique to the individuals who feel them; what sets CrimethInc. apart is that it is a means of *interlocking* these desires, of creating mutually beneficial relationships between people with different needs. This is why we have the bureaucrats and entrepreneurs, whose very existence depends on our isolation and frustration, shaking in their loafers. This is how we have come to be the ones to fire the first shots of the third and final world war, the war which will be fought for total liberation.

What is CrimethInc.?

CrimethInc. is the black market where brilliant schemes and wild abandon are traded for lives.

CrimeThink for Yourself!

How To Use This Book.
It is crucial to point out that this book isn't designed to be used in the way a "normal" book is. Rather than reading it from one cover to the other, casting perfunctory votes of disapproval or agreement along the way (or even deciding to "buy in" to our ideas, in passive consumer fashion), and then putting it on the shelf as another inert possession, we hope you will use this as a *tool* in your own efforts—not just to think about the world, but also to *change* it. This book is composed of ideas and images we've remorselessly stolen and adjusted to our purposes, and we hope you'll do exactly the same with its contents. There's no need to even read it as one unit if it doesn't please you; such a thing might be too repetitive for the average bear, anyway. But please by all means use the images for posters, take sentences for your own writing, reinterpret ideas and claim them as your own inventions, turn in the articles as papers for your Sociology class—if you must turn those papers in, that is!

As for the contents themselves: we've limited ourselves for the most part here to criticism of the established order, because we trust you to do the rest. Heaven is a different place for everyone; hell, at least this particular one, we inhabit in common. This book is supposed to help you analyze and disassemble this world—what you build for yourself in its place is in your hands, although we've offered some general ideas of where to start. In our next book we'll provide some more detailed suggestions, and share some of our experiences exploring the alternatives to the structures and forces we assault in this one. In the meantime, remember: the destructive impulse is also a creative one . . . happy smashing!

Against practicality we therefore disdain the example and admonition of tradition in order to invent at any cost something which <u>everyone</u> considers crazy!

                              -Nadia C.

Forward!

by NietzsChe Guevara

I. Normal?

People from the (rapidly splintering) "mainstream" of society in Europe and the United States today take a peculiar pleasure in considering themselves "normal" in comparison to legal offenders, political radicals, and other members of social outgroups. They treat this "normalcy" as if it is an indication of mental health and moral righteousness, regarding the "others" with a mixture of pity and disgust. But if we consult history, we can see that the conditions and patterns of human life have changed so much in the past two centuries that it is impossible to speak of *any* lifestyle available to human beings today as being "normal" in the natural sense, as being a lifestyle for which we adapted over many generations. Of the lifestyles from which a young woman growing up in the West today can choose, none are anything like the ones for which her ancestors were prepared by centuries of natural selection and evolution.

It is more likely that the "normalcy" that these people hold so dear is rather the *feelings* of normalcy that result from conformity to a standard. Being surrounded by others who behave the same way, who are conditioned to the same routines and expectations, is comforting because it reinforces the idea that one is pursuing the right course: if a great many people make the same decisions and live according to the same customs, then these decisions and customs must be the right ones.

But the mere fact that a number of people live and act in a certain way does not make it any more likely that this way of living is the one that will bring them the most happiness. Besides, the lifestyles associated with the American and European "mainstream" (if such a thing truly exists) were not exactly consciously chosen as the best possible ones by those who pursue them; rather, they came to be suddenly, as the results of technological and cultural upheavals. Once the peoples of Europe, the United States, and the world realize that there is nothing necessarily "normal" about their "normal life," they can begin to ask themselves the first and most important question of the new century:

Are there ways of thinking, acting, and living that might be more satisfying and exciting than the ways we think, act, and live today?

II. Transformation

If the accumulated knowledge of Western civilization has anything of value to offer us at this point, it is an awareness of just how much is *possible* when it comes to human life. Our otherwise foolish scholars of history and sociology and anthropology can at least show us this one thing: that human beings have lived in a thousand different kinds of societies, with ten thousand different tables of values, ten thousand different relationships to each other and the world around them, ten thousand different conceptions of self. A little traveling can still show you the same thing, if you get there before Coca-Cola has had too much of a head start.

That's why I can't help but scoff when someone refers to "human nature," invariably in the course of excusing himself for a miserable

... to live as the subject, rather than the object, of history—

resignation to our supposed fate. Don't you realize we share a common ancestor with *sea urchins?* If differing environments can make these distant cousins of ours so very distant from us, how much more possible must small changes in ourselves and our interactions be! If there is anything lacking (and there sorely, sorely is, most will admit) in our lives, anything unnecessarily tragic or meaningless in them, any corner of happiness that we have not yet thoroughly explored, then all that is needed is for us to alter our environments accordingly. "If you want to change the world, you first must change yourself," the saying goes; we have learned that the opposite is true.

And there is another valuable discovery our species has made, albeit the hard way: we are capable of absolutely transforming environments. The place you lie, sit, or stand reading this was probably altogether different a hundred years ago, not to mention two thousand years ago; and almost all of those changes were brought about by human beings. We have completely remade our world in the past few centuries, changing life for almost every kind of plant and animal, ourselves most of all. It only remains for us to experiment with executing (or, for that matter, *not* executing) these changes *intentionally*, in accordance with our needs and desires, rather than at the mercy of irrational, inhuman forces like competition, superstition, routine.

Once we realize this, we can claim a new destiny for ourselves, both individually and collectively. No longer will we be buffeted about by powers that seem beyond our control; instead, in this exploration of ourselves through the creation of new environments, we will learn all that we can be. This path will take us out of the world as we know it, far beyond the farthest horizons we can see from here. We will become artists of the grandest kind, painting with desire as a medium, deliberately creating and recreating ourselves—becoming, *ourselves,* our own greatest work.

To accomplish this, we'll need to learn how to coexist and collaborate successfully: to see just how interconnected all our lives are, and finally learn to live with that in mind. Until this becomes possible, each of us will not only be denied the vast potential of her fellows, but her own potential as well; for we all make together the world that each of us must live in and be made by.

The other thing that is lacking is the knowledge of our own desires. Desire is a slippery thing, amoebic and difficult to pin down, let alone keep up with. If we're going to make a destiny out of the pursuit and transformation of desire, we first must find ways to discover and

—or, better, as sovereign rather than subject ...

release our loves and lusts. For this, not enough experience and adventure could ever suffice. So the makers of this new world must be more generous and more greedy than any who have come before: more generous with each other, and more greedy for life!

III. Utopia

Even from here, I can taste the question already on the tip of your tongue: isn't this utopian?

Well, of course it is. You know what everyone's greatest fear is? It is that all the dreams we have, all the crazy ideas and aspirations, all the impossible romantic longings and utopian visions *can* come true, that the world *can* grant our wishes. People spend their lives doing everything in their power to fend off that possibility: they beat themselves up with every kind of insecurity, sabotage their own efforts, undermine love affairs and cry sour grapes before the world even has a chance to defeat them . . . because no weight could be heavier to bear than the possibility that everything we want *is* possible. If that is true, then there really are things at stake in this life, things to be truly won or lost. Nothing could be more heartbreaking than to fail when such success is actually possible, so we do everything we can to avoid trying in the first place, to avoid having to try.

For if there is even the slightest possibility that our hearts' desires could be realized, then of course the only thing that makes sense is to throw ourselves entirely into their pursuit and risk that heartbreak. Despair and nihilism seem safer, projecting our hopelessness onto the cosmos as an excuse for not even trying. So we remain, clutching our resignation, as secure as corpses in coffins ("better safe *and* sorry") . . . but this still cannot ward off that dreadful possibility. Thus in our hopeless flight from the real tragedy of the world, we only heap upon ourselves false tragedy, unnecessary tragedy, as well.

Perhaps this world will never conform perfectly to our needs—people will always die before they are ready, perfect relationships will end in ruins, adventures will end in catastrophe and beautiful moments be forgotten. But what breaks my heart is the way we flee from those inevitable truths into the arms of more horrible things. It may be true that every man is lost in a universe that is fundamentally indifferent to him, locked forever in a terrifying solitude—but it doesn't have to be true that some people starve while others destroy food or leave fertile farms untilled. It doesn't have to be true that men and women waste their lives away working to serve the hollow greed of a few rich men, just to survive. It doesn't have to be that we never dare to tell each other what we really want, to share ourselves honestly, to use our talents and capabilities to make life more bearable, let alone more beautiful. That's *unnecessary* tragedy, stupid tragedy, pathetic and pointless. It's not even utopian to demand that we put an end to farces like these.

If we could bring ourselves to believe, to really *feel*, the possibility that we *are* invincible and can accomplish whatever we want in this world, it wouldn't seem out of our reach at all to correct such absurdities. What I am begging you to do here is not to put faith in the impossible, but have the courage to face that terrible possibility that our lives really *are* in our own hands, and to act accordingly: to not settle for every misery fate and humanity have heaped upon us, but to push back, to see which ones can be shaken off. Nothing could be more tragic, and more ridiculous, than to live out a whole life in reach of heaven without ever stretching out your arms.

I. A Short "History" of the C.W.C.

Actually, there is nothing we despise more than history. Nothing could be more crippling than the feeling that we are part of a *chain* of events, an inescapable chain reaction that predetermines everything we do, everything that is possible. With everything around us supposedly a part of this vast continuum, it's easy to forget that history itself is actually a very recent invention.

Remember, the human race has existed for over a hundred thousand years, so it is the past few thousand years of "civilization" that are the deviation from the "natural" if anything is. Before time was divided into past and future, and then subdivided and subsubdivided further until it seems to speed past without even pausing for us to climb on, we experienced it in a radically different manner. In prehistoric days, time was not linear: it could begin afresh as the sun rose on a beautiful spring morning, pause for an eternity as your lover kissed and nibbled your thighs, end abruptly upon the death of your child. It repeated itself in circular cycles, or in climbing spirals of recurrence endlessly renewed and unique. It could not trap you or bypass you, only carry you to the moment and release you into it. Just as there were no national borders or trends of global standardization, time was not bound by any one law or system. One could trek a few days out of one's homeland and enter entirely new worlds, traveling through space and time in ways that simply couldn't be measured.

You may have noticed that while the moments of great upheaval and suffering in your life are burned into your memory forever, your experiences of bliss seem to slip through the net: while you can recall the superficial details, the actual sensations seem to melt together with those of every other experience of pleasure you can recall. This is not because happiness itself is a generic, formless condition; rather, ecstasy and pleasure are simply part of a world that lies beyond the pale of history. History cannot capture or describe the things that make life magical and precious—these things can only be approached in person. They are as invisible to hindsight and narrative as they are to the instruments of the scientist.

Read this, then, not as a *history* of CrimethInc. and its progenitors, but as an illustration in negative space, a map to places in the occupied time of our past in which *real life* surfaced for a moment—to remind us that some day it will be back forever.

To follow free spirits, turn to page 42

II. Important Documents: a CrimethInc.

Contra'd

Building (n) –
An ... vice for the production of an unlimited number of envir-... single piece of land.

...slave to rais[e] your kids, cook and clea[n] the house...

Feminism (n)
Your mother slaved over the distaff every day of her godforsaken life. So dress in a suit and get a fifty hour a week salary posi- tion so you can...

I knew an old lady who swal- lowed a fly, don't know w... she swallowe[d] a fly, I gues[s] she'll die...

Pepsi (n)
Worthles[s] things are th[e] best commodi- ties becaus[e] their price[s] are indisput- able.

symptom (n) - ... nce we had ... "in trouble" ... haracteris ... ics, how we ... ptoms

hurt, now we get "in trouble"

time (n) - ... earn from the ast, so you an use the resent to repare for he future. ... nen, one day ... e future ar ... ves and, in ... n instant, is ... one forever

wealth (n) - there are many people who pose threat and many ways of dealing with them. Some are enslaved, some put in jail, some are shot, others are starved, but the most in-

rouble (n) - ... used to ...

Note: When reading dry political theory, such as the texts you will find on the following pages, it may be useful to apply the Exclamation Point Test from time to time, to determine if the material you are reading is actually relevant to your life. To apply this test, simply go through the text replacing all the punctuation marks at the ends of sentences with exclamation points. If the results sound absurd when read aloud, then you know you're wasting your time.

is for Anarchy

The gods die twice—   *—once in heaven, once on earth.*

NO GODS NO MASTERS

AN INTRODUCTION TO THE IDEA OF THINKING FOR YOURSELF

No Gods

Once, flipping through a book on child psychology, I came across a chapter about adolescent rebellion. It suggested that in the first phase of a child's youthful rebellion against her parents, she may attempt to distinguish herself from them by accusing them of not living up to their own values. For example, if they taught her that kindness and consideration are important, she will accuse them of not being compassionate enough. In this case the child has not yet defined herself or her own values; she still accepts the values and ideas that her parents passed on to her, and she is only able to assert her identity inside of that framework. It is only later, when she questions the very beliefs and morals that were presented to her as gospel, that she can become a free-standing individual.

Far too many of us so-called radicals and revolutionaries show no signs of going beyond that first stage of rebellion. We criticize the actions of those in the mainstream and the effects of their society upon people and animals, we attack the ignorance and cruelty of their system, but we rarely stop to question the nature of what we all accept as "morality." Could it be that this "morality," by which we think we can judge their actions, is itself something that should be criticized? When we claim that the exploitation of animals is "morally wrong," what does that mean? Are we perhaps just accepting their values and turning these values against them, rather than creating moral standards of our own?

Maybe right now you're saying to yourself "what do you mean, create moral standards of our own? Something is either morally right or it isn't—morality isn't something you can make up, it's not a matter of mere opinion." Right there, you're accepting one of the most basic tenets of the society that raised you: that right and wrong are not individual valuations, but fundamental laws of the world. This idea, a holdover from a deceased Christianity, is at the center of our civilization. If you are going to question the establishment, you should question it first!

Where does the idea of "Moral Law" come from?

Once upon a time, almost everyone believed in the existence of God. This God ruled over the world, He had absolute power over everything in it; and He had set down laws which all human beings had to obey. If they did not, they would suffer the most terrible of punishments at His hands. Naturally, most people obeyed the laws as well as they could, their fear of eternal suffering being stronger than their desire for anything forbidden. Because everyone lived according to the same laws, they could agree upon what "morality" was: it was

the set of values decreed by God's laws. Thus, good and evil, right and wrong, were decided by the authority of God, which everyone accepted out of fear.

One day, people began to wake up and realize that there was no such thing as God after all. There was no hard evidence to demonstrate his existence, and few people could see any point in having faith in the irrational any longer. God pretty much disappeared from the world; nobody feared him or his punishments anymore.

But a strange thing happened. Though these people had the courage to question God's existence, and even deny it to the ones who still believed in it, they didn't dare to question the morality that His laws had mandated. Perhaps it just didn't occur to them; everyone had been raised to hold the same beliefs about what was moral, and had come to speak about right and wrong in the same way, so maybe they just assumed it was obvious what was good and what was evil whether God was there to enforce it or not. Or perhaps people had become so used to living under these laws that they were afraid to even consider the possibility that the laws didn't exist any more than God did.

This left humanity in an unusual position: though there was no longer an authority to decree certain things absolutely right or wrong, they still accepted the idea that some things were right or wrong by nature. Though they no longer had faith in a deity, they still had faith in a universal moral code that everyone had to follow. Though they no longer believed in God, they were not yet courageous enough to stop obeying His orders; they had abolished the idea of a divine ruler, but not the divinity of His code of ethics. This unquestioning submission to the laws of a long-departed heavenly master has been a long nightmare from which the human race is only just beginning to awaken.

God is dead—and with him, Moral Law.

Without God, there is no longer any objective standard by which to judge good and evil. This realization was very troubling to philosophers a few decades ago, but it hasn't really had much of an effect in other circles. Most people still seem to think that a universal morality can be grounded in something other than God's laws: in what is good for people, in what is good for society, in what we feel called upon to do. But explanations of why these standards necessarily constitute "universal moral law" are hard to come by. Usually, the arguments for the existence of moral law are emotional rather than rational: "But don't *you* think rape is wrong?" moralists ask, as if a shared opinion were a proof of universal truth. "But don't you think people need to believe in something greater than themselves?" they appeal, as if needing to believe in something can make it true. Occasionally, they even

Everything that glorifies "God" and the afterworld slanders humanity and the real world.

resort to threats: "but what would happen if everyone decided that there is no good or evil? Wouldn't we all kill each other?"

The real problem with the idea of universal moral law is that it asserts the existence of something that we have no way to know anything about. Believers in good and evil would have us believe that there are "moral truths"—that is, there are things that are morally true of this world, in the same way that it is true that the sky is blue. They claim that it is true of this world that murder is morally wrong just as it is true that water freezes at thirty two degrees. But we can investigate the freezing temperature of water: we can measure it and agree together that we have arrived at some kind of "objective" truth, insofar as such a thing is possible. On the other hand, what do we observe if we want to investigate whether it is true that murder is evil? There is no tablet of moral law on a mountaintop for us to consult, there are no commandments carved into the sky above us; all we have to go on are our own instincts and the words of a bunch of priests and other self-appointed moral experts, many of whom don't even agree. As for the words of the priests and moralists, if they can't offer any hard evidence from this world, why should we believe their claims? And regarding our instincts—if we feel that something is right or wrong, that may make it right or wrong for us, but that's not proof that it is *universally* good or evil. Thus, the idea that there are universal moral laws is mere superstition: it is a claim that things exist in this world which we can never actually experience or learn anything about. And we would do well not to waste our time wondering about things we can never know anything about.

When two people fundamentally disagree over what is right or wrong, there is no way to resolve the debate. There is nothing in this world to which they can refer to see which one is correct—because there really are no universal moral laws, just personal evaluations. So the only important question is where your values come from: do you create them yourself, according to your own desires, or do you accept them from someone else . . . someone else who has disguised *their* opinions as "universal truths"?

Haven't you always been a little suspicious of the idea of universal moral truths, anyway? This world is filled with groups and individuals who want to convert you to their religions, their dogmas, their political agendas, their opinions. Of course they will tell you that one set of values is true for everybody, and of course they will tell you that their values are the correct ones. Once you're convinced that there is only one standard of right and wrong, they're only a step away from convincing you that their standard is the right one. How carefully we should approach those who would sell us the idea of "universal moral law," then! Their claim that morality is a matter of universal law is at base just a devious way to get us to accept their values, rather than forging values of our own which might conflict with theirs.

So, to protect ourselves from the superstitions of the moralists and the trickery of the evangelists, let us be done with the idea of moral law. Let us step forward into a new era, in which we will make values of our own rather than accepting moral laws out of fear and obedience. Let this be our new creed:

There is no universal moral code that should dictate human behavior. There is no such thing as good or evil, there is no universal standard of right and wrong. Our values and morals come from us and belong to us, whether we like it or not; so we should claim them proudly for ourselves, as our own creations, rather than seeking some external justification for them.

But if there's no good or evil, if nothing has any intrinsic moral value, how do we know what to do?

Make your own good and evil. If there is no moral law standing over us, that means we're free—free to do whatever we want, free to be whatever we want, free to pursue our desires without feeling any guilt or shame about them. Figure out what it is you want in your life, and go for it; create whatever values are right for you, and live by them. It won't be easy, by any means; desires pull in different directions, they come and go without warning, so keeping up with them and choosing among them is a difficult task—of course obeying instructions is easier, less complicated. But if we just live our lives as we have been instructed to, the chances are very slim that we will get what we want out of life: each of us is different and has different needs, so how could one set of "moral truths" work for each of us? If we take responsibility for ourselves and each carve our own table of values, then we will have a fighting chance of attaining some measure of happiness. The old moral laws are left over from days when we lived in fearful submission to a nonexistent God, anyway; with their departure, we can rid ourselves of all the cowardice, submission, and superstition that has characterized our past.

Some misunderstand the claim that we should pursue our own desires to be mere hedonism. But it is not the fleeting, insubstantial desires of the typical libertine that we are speaking about here. It is the strongest, deepest, most lasting desires and inclinations of the individual: it is her most fundamental loves and hates that should shape her values. And the fact that there is no God to demand that we love one another or act virtuously does not mean that we should not do these things for our own sake, if we find them rewarding—which almost all of us do. But let us do what we do for our *own* sake, not out of obedience!

But how can we justify acting on our ethics, if we can't base them on universal moral truths?

Morality has been justified externally for so long that today we hardly know how to conceive of it in any other way. We have always had to claim that our values proceeded from something external to us, because basing values on our own desires was (not surprisingly!) branded evil by the preachers of moral law. Today we still feel instinctively that our actions must be justified by something outside of ourselves, something "greater" than ourselves—if not by God, then by moral law, state law, public opinion, justice, "love of man," etc. We have been so conditioned by centuries of asking permission to feel things and do things, of being forbidden to base any decisions on our own needs, that we still want to think we are obeying a higher power even when we act on our own desires and beliefs; somehow, it seems more defensible to act out of submission to some kind of authority than in the service of our own inclinations. We feel so ashamed of our aspirations and desires that we would rather attribute our actions to something "higher." But what could be greater than our own desires, what could possibly provide better justification for our actions? Should we be serving something external without consulting our desires, perhaps even serving *against* our desires?

This question of justification is where so many otherwise radical individuals and groups have gone wrong. They attack what they see as injustice not on the grounds that they don't want to see such things happen, but on the grounds that it is "morally wrong." By doing so, they seek the support of everyone who still believes in the fable of moral law, and they get to see themselves as servants of the Truth. These people should not be taking advantage of popular delusions to make their points, but should be challenging assumptions and questioning traditions in *everything* they do. An improvement in, for example, animal rights, which is achieved in the name of justice and morality, is a step forward at the cost of two steps back: it solves one problem while reproducing and reinforcing another. Certainly such improvements could be fought for and attained on the grounds that they are *desirable* (nobody who truly considered it would really *want* to needlessly slaughter and mistreat animals, would they?), rather than with tactics leftover from Christian superstition. Unfortunately, because of centuries of conditioning, it feels so good to feel justified by some "higher force," to be obeying "moral law," to be enforcing "justice" and fighting "evil" that it's easy for people get caught up in their role as moral enforcers and forget to question whether the idea of moral law makes sense in the first place. There is a sensation of power that comes from believing that one is serving a higher authority, the same one that attracts people to fascism. It's always tempting to paint any struggle as good against evil, right against wrong; but that is not just an oversimplification, it is a falsification: for no such things exist.

We can act compassionately towards each other because we *want* to, not just because "morality dictates," you know! We don't need any justification from above to care about animals and humans, or to act

to protect them. We need only feel in our hearts that it is right, that it is right for *us*, to have all the reason we need. Thus we can justify acting on our ethics, without basing them on moral truths, simply by not being ashamed of our desires: by being proud enough of them to accept them for what they are, as the forces that drive us as individuals. And our own values might not be right for everyone, it's true; but they are all each of us has to go on, so we should dare to act on them rather than wishing for some impossible greater justification.

But what would happen if everyone decided that there is no good or evil? Wouldn't we all kill each other?

This question presupposes that people refrain from killing each other only because they have been taught that it is evil to do so. Is humanity really so absolutely bloodthirsty and vicious that we would all rape and kill each other if we weren't restrained by superstition? It seems more likely to me that we desire to get along with each other at least as much as we desire to be destructive—don't you usually enjoy helping others more than you enjoy hurting them? Today, most people claim to believe that compassion and fairness are morally right, but this has done little to make the world into a compassionate and fair place. Might it not be true that we would act upon our natural inclinations to human decency more, rather than less, if we did not feel that charity and justice were obligatory? What would it really be worth, anyway, if we did all fulfill our "duty" to be good to each other, if it was only because we were obeying moral imperatives? Wouldn't it mean a lot more for us to treat each other with consideration because we *want* to, rather than because we feel required to?

And if the abolition of the myth of moral law somehow causes more strife between human beings, won't that still be better than living as slaves to superstitions? If we make our own minds up about what our values are and how we will live according to them, we at least will have the chance to pursue our desires and perhaps enjoy life, even if we have to struggle against each other. But if we choose to live according to rules set for us by others, we sacrifice the chance to choose our destinies and pursue our dreams. No matter how smoothly we might get along in the shackles of moral law, is it worth the abdication of our self determination? I wouldn't have the heart to lie to a fellow human being and tell him he had to conform to some ethical mandate whether it was in his best interest or not, even if that lie would prevent a conflict between us. Because I care about human beings, I want them to be free to do what is right for them. Isn't that more important than mere peace on earth? Isn't freedom, even dangerous freedom, preferable to the safest slavery, to peace bought with ignorance, cowardice, and submission?

The wages of sin are freedom.

Besides, look back at our history. So much bloodshed, deception, and oppression have already been perpetrated in the name of right and wrong. The bloodiest wars have been fought between opponents who each thought they were fighting on the side of moral truth. The idea of moral law doesn't help us get along, it turns us against each other, to contend over whose moral law is the "true" one. There can be no real progress in human relations until everyone's perspectives on ethics and values are acknowledged; then we can finally begin to work out our differences and learn to live together, without fighting over the absolutely stupid question of whose values and desires are "right." For your own sake, for the sake of humanity, cast away the antiquated notions of good and evil and create your values for yourself!

No Masters

If you liked school, you'll love work. The cruel, absurd abuses of power, the self-satisfied authority that the teachers and principals lorded over you, the intimidation and ridicule of your classmates don't end at graduation. Those things are all present in the adult world, only more so. If you thought you lacked freedom before, wait until you have to answer to shift leaders, managers, owners, landlords, creditors, tax collectors, city councils, draft boards, law courts, and police. When you get out of school you may escape the jurisdiction of some authorities, but you enter the control of even more domineering ones. Do you enjoy being controlled by others who don't understand or care about your wants and needs? Do you get anything out of obeying the instructions of employers, the restrictions of landlords, the laws of magistrates, people who have powers over you that you would never have given them willingly?

How is it that they get all this power, anyway? The answer is *hierarchy*.

Hierarchy is a value system in which your worth measured by the number of people and things you control, and how dutifully you obey those above you. Weight is exerted downward through the power structure: everyone is forced to accept and conform to this system by everyone else. You're afraid to disobey those above you because they can bring to bear against you the power of everyone and everything under them. You're afraid to abdicate your power over those below you because they might end up above you. In our hierarchical system, we're all so busy trying to protect ourselves from each other that we never have a chance to stop and ask if this is really the best way our society could be organized. If we could think about it, we'd probably agree that it isn't; for we all know happiness comes from control over our own lives, not other people's lives. And as long as we're busy competing for control over others, we're bound to be the victims of control ourselves.

It is our hierarchical system that teaches us from childhood to accept the power of any authority figure, regardless of whether it is in

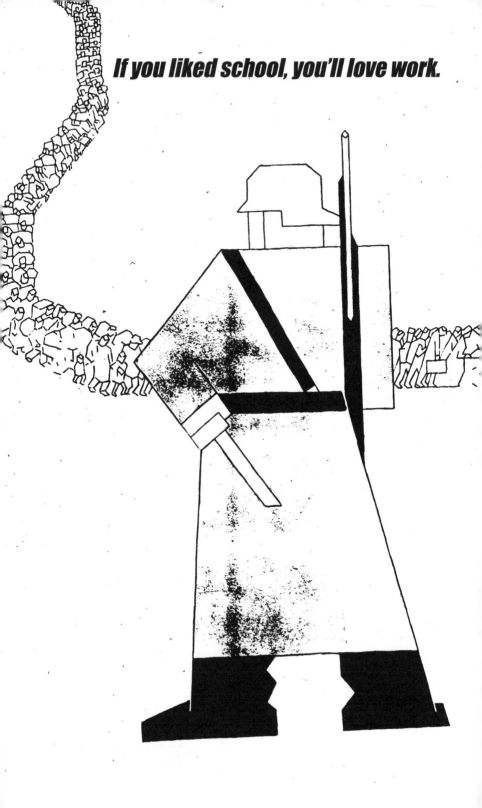

our best interest or not. We learn to bow instinctively before anyone who claims to be more important than we are. It is hierarchy that makes homophobia common among poor people in the U.S.A.— they're desperate to feel more valuable, more significant than *somebody*. It is hierarchy at work when two hundred punk rockers go to a rock club (already a mistake, of course!) to see a band, and for some stupid reason the clubowner won't let them perform: there are two hundred and six people at the club, two hundred and five of whom want the band to play, but they all accept the decision of the clubowner just because he is older and owns the place (i.e. has more financial power, and thus more legal power). It is hierarchical values that are responsible for racism, classism, sexism, and a thousand other prejudices that are deeply ingrained in our society. It is hierarchy that makes rich people look at poor people as if they aren't even human, and vice versa. It pits employer against employee, manager against worker, teacher against student, making people struggle against each other rather than work together in mutual aid; separated this way, they can't benefit from each other's skills and ideas and abilities, but must live in jealousy and fear of them. It is hierarchy at work when your boss insults you or makes sexual advances at you and you can't do anything about it, just as it is when police flaunt their power over you. For power does make people cruel and heartless, and submission does make people cowardly and stupid: and most people in a hierarchical system partake in both. Hierarchical values are responsible for our destruction of the natural environment and the exploitation of animals: led by the capitalist West, our species seeks control over anything we can get our claws on, at any cost to ourselves or others. And it is hierarchical values that send us to war, fighting for power over each other, inventing more and more powerful weapons until finally the whole world teeters on the edge of nuclear annihilation.

But what can we do about hierarchy? Isn't that just the way the world works? Or are there other ways that people could interact, other values we could live by?

Hierarchy . . .

Resurrecting anarchism as a personal approach to life.

Stop thinking of anarchism as just another "world order," just another social system. From where we all stand, in this very dominated, very controlled world, it is impossible to imagine living without any authorities, without laws or governments. No wonder anarchism isn't usually taken seriously as a large-scale political or social program: no one can imagine what it would really be like, let alone how to achieve it—not even the anarchists themselves.

Instead, think of anarchism as an individual orientation to yourself and others, as a personal approach to life. That's not impossible to imagine. Conceived in these terms, what would anarchism be? It would be a decision to think for yourself rather than following blindly. It would be a rejection of hierarchy, a refusal to accept the "god given" authority of any nation, law, or other force as being more significant than your own authority over yourself. It would be an instinctive distrust of those who claim to have some sort of rank or status above the others around them, and an unwillingness to claim such status over others for yourself. Most of all, it would be a refusal to place responsibility for yourself in the hands of others: it would be the demand that each of us not only be able to choose our own destiny, but also do so.

According to this definition, there are a great deal more anarchists than it seemed, though most wouldn't refer to themselves as

& Anarchy

such. For most people, when they think about it, want to have the right to live their own lives, to think and act as they see fit. Most people trust themselves to figure out what they should do more than they trust any authority to dictate it to them. Almost everyone is frustrated when they find themselves pushing against faceless, impersonal power.

You don't want to be at the mercy of governments, bureaucracies, police, or other outside forces, do you? Surely you don't let them dictate your entire life. Don't you do what you want to, what you believe in, at least whenever you can get away with it? In our everyday lives, we all are anarchists. Whenever we make decisions for ourselves, whenever we take responsibility for our own actions rather than deferring to some higher power, we are putting anarchism into practice.

So if we are all anarchists by nature, why do we always end up accepting the domination of others, even creating forces to rule over us? Wouldn't you rather figure out how to coexist with your fellow human beings by working it out directly between yourselves, rather than depending on some external set of rules? The system *they* accept is the one *you* must live under: if you want your freedom, you can't afford to not be concerned about whether those around you demand control of their lives or not.

Do we really need masters to command and control us?

In the West, for thousands of years, we have been sold centralized state power and hierarchy in general on the premise that we do. We've all been taught that without police, we would all kill each other; that without bosses, no work would ever get done; that without governments, civilization itself would fall to pieces. Is all this true?

Certainly, it's true that today little work gets done when the boss isn't watching, chaos ensues when governments fall, and violence sometimes occurs when the police aren't around. But are these really indications that there is no other way we could organize society?

Isn't it possible that workers won't get anything done unless they are under observation because they are used to not doing anything without being prodded—more than that, because they resent being inspected, instructed, condescended to by their managers, and don't want to do anything for them that they don't have to? Perhaps if they were working together for a common goal, rather than being paid to take orders, working towards objectives that they have no say in and that don't interest them much, they would be more proactive. Not to say that everyone is ready or able to do such a thing today; but our laziness is conditioned rather than natural, and in a different environment, we might find that people don't need bosses to get things done.

And as for police being necessary to maintain the peace: we won't discuss the ways in which the role of "law enforcer" brings out the most brutal aspects of human beings, and how police brutality doesn't exactly contribute to peace. How about the effects on civilians living in a police-"protected" state? Once the police are no longer a direct manifestation of the desires of the community they serve (and that happens quickly, whenever a police force is established: they become a power external to the rest of society, an outside authority), they are a force acting coercively on the people of that society. Violence isn't just limited to physical harm: any relationship that is established by force, such as the one between police and civilians, is a violent relationship. When you are acted upon violently, you learn to act violently back. Isn't it possible, then, that the implicit threat of police on every street corner—of the near omnipresence of uniformed, impersonal representatives of state power—contributes to tension and violence, rather than dispelling them? If that doesn't seem likely to you, and you are middle class and/or white, ask a poor black or Hispanic man how the presence of police makes *him* feel.

I awoke in a sweat from the American Dream

When the standard forms of human interaction all revolve around hierarchical power, when human intercourse so often comes down to giving and receiving orders (at work, at school, in the family, in the courts), how can we expect to have no violence in our society? People are used to using force against each other in their daily lives, the force of authoritarian power; of course using physical force cannot be far behind in such a system. Perhaps if we were more used to treating each other as equals, to creating relationships based upon equal concern for each other's needs, we wouldn't see so many people resort to physical violence against each other.

And what about government control? Without it, would our society fall into pieces, and our lives with it?

Certainly, things would be a great deal different without governments than they are now—but is that necessarily a bad thing? Is our modern society really the best of all possible worlds? Is it worth it to grant masters and rulers so much control over our lives, out of fear of trying anything different?

Besides, we can't claim that we need government control to prevent mass bloodshed, because it is governments that have carried out the greatest slaughters of all: in wars, in holocausts, in the centrally organized enslavement and obliteration of entire peoples and cultures. And it may be that when governments break down, many people lose their lives in the resulting chaos and infighting. But this fighting is almost always between other power-hungry hierarchical groups, other would-be governors and rulers. If we were to reject hierarchy absolutely, and refuse to serve any force above ourselves, there would no longer be any large scale wars or holocausts. That would be a responsibility each of us would have to take on equally, to collectively refuse to recognize any power as worth serving, to swear allegiance to nothing but ourselves and our fellow human beings. If we all were to do that, we would never see another world war again.

Of course, even if a world entirely without hierarchy is possible, we should not have any illusions that any of us will live to see it realized. That should not even be our concern: for it is foolish to arrange your life so that it revolves around something that you will never be able to experience. We should, rather, recognize the patterns of submission and domination in our own lives, and, to the best of our ability, break free of them. We should put the anarchist ideal—no masters, no slaves—into effect in our daily lives however we can. Every time one of us remembers not to accept at face value the authority of the powers that be, each time one of us is able to escape the system of domination for a moment (whether it is by getting away with something forbidden by a teacher or boss, relating to a member of a different social stratum as an equal, etc.), that is a victory for the individual and a blow against hierarchy.

Do you still believe that a hierarchy-free society is impossible? There are plenty of examples throughout human history: the bushmen of the Kalahari desert still live without authorities, never trying to force or command each other to do things, but working together and granting each other freedom and autonomy. Sure, their society is being destroyed by our more warlike one—but that isn't to say that an egalitarian society could not exist that was extremely hostile to, and well-defended against, the encroachments of external power! In *Cities of the Red Night*, William Burroughs writes about an anarchist pirates' stronghold a few hundred years ago that was just that.

If you need an example closer to your daily life, remember the last time you gathered with your friends to relax on a Friday night. Some of you brought food, some of you brought entertainment, some provided other things, but nobody kept track of who owed what to whom. You did things as a group and enjoyed yourselves; things actually got done, but nobody was forced to do anything, and nobody assumed the position of master. We have these moments of non-capitalist, non-coercive, non-hierarchical interaction in our lives constantly, and these are the times when we most enjoy the company of others, when we get the most out of other people; but somehow it doesn't occur to us to demand that our society work this way, as well as our friendships and love affairs. Sure, it's a lofty goal to ask that it does— but let's dare to reach for high goals, let's not settle for anything less than the best in our lives!

"Anarchism" is the revolutionary idea that no one is more qualified than you are to decide what your life will be.

—It means trying to figure out how to work *together* to meet our individual needs, how to work *with* each other rather than "for" or against each other. And when this is impossible, it means preferring strife to submission and domination.

—It means not valuing any system or ideology above the people it purports to serve, not valuing anything theoretical above the *real things* in this world. It means being faithful to real human beings (and animals, etc.), fighting for ourselves and for each other, not out of "responsibility," not for "causes" or other intangible concepts.

—It means not forcing your desires into a hierarchical order, either, but accepting and embracing all of them, accepting yourself. It means not trying to force the self to abide by any external laws, not trying to restrict your emotions to the predictable or the practical, not pushing your instincts and desires into boxes: for there is no cage large enough to accommodate the human soul in all its flights, all its heights and depths.

—It means refusing to put the responsibility for your happiness in anyone else's hands, whether that be parents, lovers, employers, or society itself. It means taking the pursuit of meaning and joy in your life upon your own shoulders.

For what else should we pursue, if not happiness? If something isn't valuable because we find meaning and joy in it, then what could possibly make it important? How could abstractions like "responsibility," "order," or "propriety" possibly be more important than the real needs of the people who invented them? Should we serve employers, parents, the State, God, capitalism, moral law, causes, movements, "society" before *ourselves? Who taught you that, anyway?*

THE BRETHREN OF THE FREE SPIRIT

cross almost two millennia, the Catholic Church maintained a stranglehold over life in Europe. It was able to do this because Christianity gave it a monopoly on the meaning of life: everything that was sacred, everything that mattered was not to be found in this world, only in another. Man was impure, profane, trapped on a worthless earth with everything beautiful forever locked beyond his reach, in heaven.[1] Only the Church could act as an intermediary to that other world, and only through it could people approach the meaning of their lives.

Mysticism was the first revolt against this monopoly: determined to experience for themselves a taste of this otherworldly beauty, mystics did whatever it took—starvation, self-flagellation, all kinds of privation—to achieve a moment of divine vision: to pay a visit to heaven, and return to tell of what blessedness awaited there. The Church grudgingly accepted the first mystics, privately outraged that anyone would sidestep its primacy in all communication with God, but believing rightly that the stories the mystics told would only reinforce the Church's claims that all value and meaning rested in another world.

But one day, a new kind of mysticism appeared; those who practiced it were generally known as the Brethren of the Free Spirit. These were men and women who had gone through the mystical process, but returned with a different story: the identification with God could be *permanent,* not just fleeting, they announced. Once they had had their transforming experience, they felt no gulf between heaven and earth, between sacred and profane, between God and man. The heretics of the Free Spirit taught that the original sin, the *only* sin, was this division of the world, which created the illusion of damnation; for since God was holy and good, and had made all things, then all things truly were wholly good, and all anyone had to do to be perfect was to make this discovery.

Thus these heretics became gods on earth: heaven was not something to strive towards, but a place they lived in; every desire they might feel was absolutely holy and beautiful, and not only that—it was the same as a divine commandment, more important than any law or custom, since all desires were created by God. In their revelation of the perfection of the world and themselves, they even were able to go beyond God, and place themselves at the center of the world: accepting the Church's authority and objective world view had meant that if God had not invented them, they would not exist; but now, accepting their own desires and perspectives as sovereign, and therefore asserting their own *subjective* experience of the world as the only authority, they were able to see that if they had not existed, then *God* would not exist.

The book of *Schwester Katrei*, one of the sources that remains from these times, describes one woman's pursuit of divinity through this kind of mysticism; at the end, she announces to her confessor, in words that shook the medieval world: "Sir, rejoice with me, for I have *become God.*"

---

[1] Even today, Christianity teaches that whatever is worthy about you is God's, and whatever is imperfect about you is your own failing—thus we have existence of our own only to the extent that we are flawed and shameful.

The Brethren of the Free Spirit were never a movement or an organized religious group; in fact, they resembled CrimethInc. more than any group since has. Their secrets were spread through the world, among people of all classes, by humble wanderers who traveled from one land to the next seeking adventure. These were vagabonds who refused to work not out of self-denial but because they proclaimed that they were too good for work, as they suggested anyone else could be who wanted to; accordingly, they declined to spend their lives selling their beliefs, as so many traditional Christians (and Communists, and even anarchists) do, but rather concentrated on *living* them—which proved, of course, to be far more infectious.

Of course the Catholic Church responded to this heresy by slaughtering the Brethren by the thousands. Anything less than a campaign of all-out terror would have sealed its fate, as its authority was almost entirely undermined by this new liberating theology. Despite the violence of this repression, however, the secrets of the Free Spirit were passed on across vast measures of time and space; they traveled unseen and uncharted, through corridors hidden to history (perhaps because they consisted of moments lived *outside* of history?), to appear in social explosions and near-revolutions hundreds of years and thousands of miles apart[2]. On many occasions the power of the

Church and the nations that served it was almost broken by these seemingly spontaneous uprisings; they appear throughout official history like a heartbeat in a sleeping body.

The heretics of the Free Spirit managed to reach a state of total self-confidence and empowerment that we anarchists and feminists only dream of today; that they managed to do this using the raw materials of Christianity, traditionally such a confining and crippling religion, is truly amazing. I often think that if only we could cast away all our doubts and inhibitions and really feel that what we are *is* beauty and perfection (*must be,* if such concepts are to exist at all!), and what we want is nothing to fear or be ashamed of, we would become invincible and the world would be ours forever more. ❀

[2] see also: the Ranters, the Diggers, the Anabaptists, the Antinomians, etc.

☞ TURN THE PAGE FOR DEVILISH CONSCIENCE RASCALS

THE PAUPER KINGS OF THE SEA

During the early seventeenth century the port city of Salè on the Moroccan coast became a haven for pirates from all over the world, eventually evolving into a free, proto-anarchist state that attracted, among others, poor, outcast Europeans who came in droves to begin new lives of piracy preying upon the trade ships of their former home countries. Among these European Renegadoes was the Dread Captain Bellamy; his hunting ground was the Straits of Gibraltar, where all ships with legitimate commerce changed course at the mention of his name, often to no avail. One Captain of a captured merchant vessel was treated to this speech by Bellamy after declining an invitation to join the pirates:

I am sorry they won't let you have your sloop again, for I scorn to do anyone a mischief, when it is not to my advantage; damn the sloop, we must sink her, and she might be of use to you. Though you are a sneaking puppy, and so are all those who submit to be governed by laws which rich men have made for their own security; for the cowardly whelps have not the courage otherwise to defend what they get by knavery; but damn ye altogether: damn them for a pack of crafty rascals, and you, who serve them, for a parcel of hen-hearted numbskulls. They vilify us, the scoundrels do, when there is only this difference, they rob the poor under the cover of law, forsooth, and we plunder the rich under protection of our own courage. Had you not better make then one of us, than sneak after these villains for employment?

When the captain replied that his conscience would not let him break the laws of God and man, the pirate Bellamy continued:

You are a devilish conscience rascal, I am a free prince, and I have as much authority to make war on the whole world as he who has a hundred sail of ships at sea, and an army of 100,000 men in the field, and this my conscience tells me; but there is no arguing with such snivelling puppies, who allow superiors to kick them about deck at pleasure.

HORUSCE en HAREADEN BARBAROSSA

FOR ANARCHY BY THE DEED, TURN TO PAGE 56

is for the Bourgeoisie

Raise the double standard of living!

the discreet charm of the

[adapted from
George Orwell's
Homage to Catatonia]

BOURGEOISIE

Or, the Tyranny of the Hair Dryer

Does your father drift from one hobby to another, fruitlessly seeking a meaningful way to spend the little "leisure time" he gets off from work? Does your mother endlessly redecorate the house, going from one room to the next until she can start over at the beginning again? Do you agonize constantly over your future, as if there was some kind of track laid out ahead you—and the world would end if you turned off of it? *If the answer to these questions is yes, it sounds like you're in the clutches of the bourgeoisie, the last barbarians on earth.*

The Martial Law of Public Opinion

Public opinion is an absolute value to the bourgeois man and woman because they know they are living in a herd: a herd of scared animals, that will turn on anyone it doesn't recognize as its own. They shiver in fear as they ponder what "the neighbors" will think of their son's new hairstyle. They plot ways to seem even more normal than their friends and coworkers. They don't dare fail to turn on their lawn sprinklers or dress appropriately for "casual Fridays" at the office. Anything that could drag them out of their routines is viewed as suspect at best. Love and lust are both diseases, possibly fatal, as are all the other passions that could drive one to do things that would result in expulsion from the flock. Keep them quarantined to secret affairs and teenage dates, to night clubs and strip clubs—for God's sake, don't contaminate the rest of us. Go wild when "your" football team wins a game, drink yourself into oblivion when the weekend comes, rent obscene movies if you have to, but don't you dare sing or run or make love out here. Under no circumstances admit to feeling anything that doesn't belong in the staff room or at the dinner party. Under no conditions admit to wanting anything more or different than what "everyone else" wants, whatever and whoever *that* might be.

And of course their children have learned this, too. Even after the death matches of the grade school nightmare, even among the most rebellious and radical of the nonconformists, the same rules are in place: don't confuse anybody as to where you stand. Don't use the wrong signifiers or subscribe to the wrong codes. Don't dance when you're supposed to be posing, don't speak when you're supposed to be dancing, don't mess with the genre or the moves. Make sure you have enough money to participate in the various rituals. To keep your identity intact, make it clear which subcultures and styles you're aligned to, which bands and fashions and politics you want to be associated with. You wouldn't dare risk your identity, would you? That's your

conform **EVEN WHEN YOU DON'T
SEE ANY** people **AROUND YOU.
THE ONE YOU DON'T SEE
MIGHT HIT YOU.**

WHEN YOU ARE detached
**DECISIONS ARE SLOWER
AND HARDER TO MAKE.**

**GOOD JUDGMENT
IS NOTHING MORE
THAN** compliance

character armor, your only protection against certain death at the hands of your friends. Without an identity, without borders to define the edges of your self, you'd just dissolve into the void . . . wouldn't you?

The Generation Gap

The older generations of the bourgeoisie have nothing to offer the younger ones because they have nothing in the first place. All their standards are hollow, all of their riches are consolation prizes, not one of their values contains any reference to real joy or fulfill-ment. Their children sense this, and rebel accordingly, whenever they can get away with it. The ones that don't have already been beaten into terrified submission.

So how has bourgeois society continued to perpetuate itself through so many generations? By absorbing this rebellion as a part of the natural life cycle. Because *every* child rebels as soon as she is old enough to have a sense of self at all, this rebellion is presented as an integral part of adolescence—and thus the woman who wants to con-tinue her rebellion into adulthood is made to feel that she is insisting on remaining a child forever. It's worth pointing out that a brief sur-vey of other cultures and peoples will reveal that this "adolescent re-bellion" is *not* inevitable or "natural."

This perpetual rebellion of the youth also creates deep gulfs between different generations of the bourgeoisie, which play a crucial role in maintaining the existence of the bourgeoisie as such. Because the adults always seem to be the enforcers of the status quo, and the youth do not have the perspective yet to see that their rebellion has also been absorbed into that status quo, generation after generation of young people are able to make the mistake of identifying older people *themselves* as the source of their misfortunes rather than realizing that these misfortunes are the result of a larger system of misery. They grow older and become bourgeois adults themselves, unable to recognize that they are merely replacing their former enemies, and still unable to bridge the so-called generation gap to learn from people of other age groups . . . let alone establish some kind of unified resistance with them. Thus the different generations of the bourgeoisie, while seemingly fighting amongst themselves, work together harmoniously as components of the larger social machine to ensure maximum alienation for all.

The Myth of the Mainstream

The bourgeois man depends upon the existence of a mythical mainstream to justify his way of life. He needs this mainstream because his social instincts are skewed in the same way his conception of democracy is: he thinks that whatever the majority is, wants, does, must be right. Nothing could be more terrifying to him than this new development, which he is beginning to sense today: that there no longer *is* a majority, if there ever was.

Our society is so fragmented, so diverse, that at this point it is absurd to speak of a "mainstream." This is a myth partly created by the anonymity of our cities. Almost everyone one passes on the street is a stranger: one mentally relegates these anonymous figures to the faceless mass one calls the mainstream, to which one attributes whatever properties one thinks of strangers as possessing (for the smug salesman, they all envy him for being even more respectable than they are; for the insecure bohemian rebel, they must disapprove of him for not being like they all are). They must be part of the silent majority, that invisible force that makes everything the way it is; one assumes that they are the same "normal people" seen in television commercials. But the fact is, of course, that those commercials refer to an unattainable ideal, in order to keep *everyone* feeling left out and insufficient. The "mainstream" is analogous to this ideal, as it keeps everyone in line without ever actually making an appearance, and possesses the same degree of reality as the perfect family in the toothpaste advertisement.

No one worries more about this absent mass than the bohemian children of the bourgeoisie. They bicker over how to orchestrate their protests to gain "mass appeal" for their radical ideas, as if there still was a mass to appeal to! Their society is now made up of *many* communities, and the only question is which communities they should approach... and dressing "nice," proper language and all, is probably *not* the best way to appeal to the most potentially revolutionary elements of their society. In the last analysis, the so-called "mainstream" audience most of them imagine they are dressing up for at their demonstrations and political events is probably just the spectre of their bourgeois parents, engraved deep in their collective unconscious (collective psychosis?) as a symbol of the adolescent insecurity and guilt they never got over. They would do better to cut their ties to the bourgeoisie entirely by feeling free to act, look, and speak in whatever ways are pleasurable, no matter who is watching—even when they are trying to advance some political cause: for no po-

litical objective reached by activists in camouflage could be more important than beginning the struggle towards a world in which people will not have to disguise themselves to be taken seriously.

This is not to pardon those insecure bohemians who use their activism not as a means of building ties with others, but rather as a way to set themselves apart: in their desperation to purchase an identity for themselves, they believe they must pay for it by defining themselves *against* others. You can recognize them by their self-righteousness, their pompous show of ideological certainty, the ostentatious way they declare themselves "activists" at every opportunity. Political "activism" is almost exclusively their sphere, today, and "exclusive" is the key word . . . until this changes, the world will not.

Marriage ... and Other Substitutes for Love and Community

Reproduction is a big issue for the bourgeois man and woman. They can only have children under very precise circumstances; anything else is "irresponsible," "unwise," "a poor decision for the future." They must be prepared to give up every last vestige of their youthful, selfish freedom to have children, for the mobility their corporations demand and the strain of vicious competition have destroyed the community network that long ago used to share the labor of child-rearing. Now every family unit is a tiny military outpost, closed and locked to the outside world both in their hearts and in the paranoia-turned-city-planning of their suburbs, each one an isolated emotional economy to itself where scarcity is the key word. The father and mother must abandon their selves for the prescribed roles of care-giver and bread-winner, for in the bourgeois world there is no other way to provide for the child. Thus the bourgeois couple's own fertility has been made a threat to their freedom, and a natural part of human life has become a social control mechanism.

Marriage and the "nuclear family" (the atomized family?) as chain gang have survived as a result of this calamity, much to the misfortune of potential lovers everywhere. For as the young adventurer, who keeps her lusts strong and her appetite whetted with constant danger and solitude, knows well, love and sexual desire cannot survive overexpo-

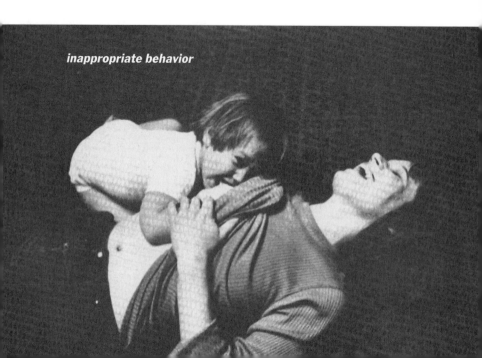

inappropriate behavior

sure—especially in the dull and lifeless settings that most married partners share time. The bourgeois husband sees the only lover he is permitted under only the worst possible circumstances: after every other force in his world has had the chance to exhaust and infuriate him for the day. The bourgeois wife learns to punish and ignore as "unrealistic" and "impractical" her every desire for romance, spontaneity, wonder. Together, they live in a hell of unfulfillment. What they need is a real community of caring people around them, so parenthood would not force them into unwanted "respectability," so they would still be free to have the individual adventures they need to keep their time together sweet, so they would never find themselves so lost and desperately lonely.

In just the same way, their steady supply of food, of conveniences, comforts, and diversions avail them not. For as every hitchhiker, every hero, every terrorist knows, these things gain their value through their *absence,* and can offer real joy only as luxuries happened upon in the pursuit of something greater. Constant access to sex, food, warmth, and shelter desensitize a man to the very pleasures they afford. The bourgeois man has given up his chance to pursue real stakes in life for the assurance that he will have these amenities and securities; but without real stakes in his life, these can offer him no more real joy than the company of his fellow prisoners.

The Joys of Surrogate Living!

You can take a quick tour of all the unacted desires of the bourgeois man just by turning on his television or stepping into one of his movie theaters. He spends as much of his time as he can in these various virtual realities because he instinctively feels that they can offer him more excitement and satisfaction than the real world. The saddest part is that, so long as he remains bourgeois, this may actually be true. And as long as he accepts the displacement of his desires into the marketplace by paying for imitations of their fulfillment, he will be trapped in the empty role that is himself.

These desires are not always pretty to see played out in Technicolor and SurroundSound: the bourgeois man's dreams and appetites are as infected by the fetishization of power and control as his society is. The closest he seems to be able to offer to an expression of free, liberated desire is the fantasy of all-consuming destruction that appears again and again at the black heart of his wildest cinematic fever dreams. This makes sense enough—after all, in a world of nothing but strip malls and theme parks, what honest thing is there to do but destroy?

The bourgeois man is not equipped to view his desires as anything but unfortunate weaknesses to be fended off with placebos, because his life has never been about the pursuit of pleasure—he has spent several centuries achieving higher and higher standards of survival, at the cost of everything else. Tonight he sits in his living room surrounded by computers, can openers, radar detectors, home entertainment systems, novelty ties, microwave dinners, and cellular phones, with no idea what went wrong.

The bourgeois man is only possible by virtue of the blinders he wears that prevent him from imagining that any other way of life is possible. As far as he can tell, everyone from the impoverished migrant workers of his own nation to the monks of Tibet would be bourgeois too, if only they could afford it. He does his damnedest to maintain these illusions; without them, he would have to face the fact that he has thrown his life away *for nothing*.

The bourgeois man is not an individual. He is not a real person (although if he was, he would probably live in Connecticut). He is a cancer inside all of us. He can now be cured.

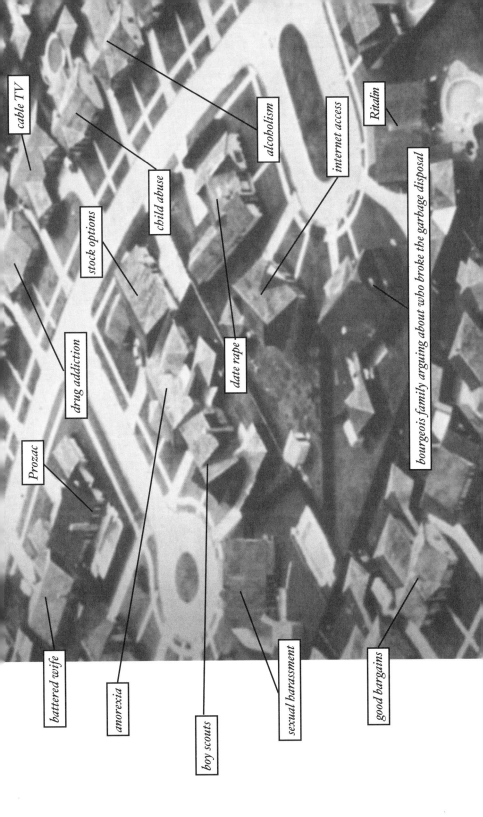

PERCY SHELLEY AND MARY GODWIN ELOPE

Percy Bysshe Shelley, a young anarchist who was to go down in history as the greatest of the Romantic poets, came to visit William Godwin, an aging writer of proto-anarchist philosophy, and ended up absconding with his daughter—showing once and for all that *even a poet knows how to turn theory into practice better than a philosopher!* ☾

A HOLIDAY WITHOUT END, PAGE 83

**is for Capitalism
and Culture**

[This article originally appeared in the form of a comic distributed to business majors at public universities across the United States. Certain scandalous parts of it were reprinted in the COINTELPRO handbook update 1998 and the Wall Street Journal, *among other publications.]*

What is capitalism, anyway?

Capitalism. That's like *democracy*, isn't it? (And aren't the enemies of capitalism the opponents of democracy? Didn't we defeat them in the Cold War?)

Actually, capitalism and democracy are two very different things. Democracy is, essentially, the idea that people should have control over their lives, that power should be shared by all rather than concentrated in the hands of a few. Capitalism is something altogether different.

In the United States (and other Western nations), we're used to hearing that we live in a democratic society. It's true that we have a *government* that calls itself democratic (although whether each of us really has an equal say, or much of a say at all, in such a bloated and atrophied "representative democracy" is worth asking), but whether our *society* is itself democratic is another question entirely. Government is only one aspect of society, of course; and it is far from the most important one, when it comes to considering day to day life. The economic system of any given society has more influence over daily life than any court or congress could: for it is economics that decides who has control over the lands, resources, and tools of the society, what people have to do each day to survive and "get ahead," and ultimately how those people interact with each other and view the world.

And capitalism is, in fact, one of the *least* democratic economic systems. In a "democratic" economy, each member of the society would have an equal say in how resources are used and how work is done. But in the capitalist economy, in which all resources are private property and everyone competes against each other for them, most resources end up under the control of a few people (today, read: corporations). Those people can decide how everyone else will work, since most of the others can't live without earning money from them. They even get to determine the physical and psychological landscape of the society, since they own most of the land and control most of the media. And at bottom, *they* aren't really in control, either, for if they let their guard down and stop working to keep ahead they will quickly be at the bottom of the pyramid with everybody else; that means *nobody* truly has freedom under the capitalist system: everyone is equally at the mercy of the laws of competition.

capital: *wealth (money, property, or labor) . . . which can be used to create more wealth. example: factory owners who profit from selling goods created by the labor of workers in their factories are able to purchase more factories.*

capitalism: *the "free exchange of goods and services" . . . in which those who have capital are able to collect more, at the expense of those who do not.*

How does capitalism work?

Here's how the free market is *supposed* to work: people are free to seek their fortunes as they choose, and the ones who work the hardest and provide the greatest value to society are rewarded with the greatest wealth. But this system has a crucial flaw: it doesn't actually offer equal opportunities for everyone. Success in the "free market" depends almost entirely on how much wealth you already have.

When capital is privately owned, an individual's opportunities to learn, work, and earn wealth are directly tied to the amount of wealth she has. A few scholarships can't offset this. It takes resources of some kind to produce something of value, and if a person doesn't have those resources herself she finds she is at the mercy of those who do. Meanwhile, those who already have those resources can make more and more wealth, and eventually most of the wealth of the society ends up in hands of a few. This leaves everyone else with little capital to sell other than their own labor, which they must sell to the capitalists (those who control most of the means of production) to survive.

This sounds confusing, but it's actually pretty simple. A corporation like Nike has plenty of extra money to open up a new shoe factory, buy new advertisements, and sell more shoes, thus earning themselves more money to invest. A poor sucker like you barely has enough money to open up a lemonade stand, and even if you did you would probably be run out of business by a larger, more established company like Pepsi which has more money to spend on promotion (sure, there are success stories of little guys triumphing over the competition, but you can see why that doesn't usually happen). Chances are you'll end up working for them if you need to earn a "living." And working for them reinforces their power: for although they pay you for your work, you can be sure they're not paying you for its full value: that's how they make a profit. If you work at a factory and you make $1000 worth of machinery parts every day, you probably only get paid $100 or less for that day's labor. That means someone is cashing in on your efforts; and the longer they do that, the more wealth and opportunities *they* have, at *your* expense.

kneel

How does this affect the average guy?

This means that your time and creative energy are being bought from you, which is the worst part of all. When all you have to sell in return for the means to survive is your own labor, you are forced to sell your life away in increments just to exist. You end up spending the greater part of your life doing whatever you can get paid the most for, instead of what you really want to do: you trade your dreams for salaries and your freedom to act for material possessions. In your "free" time you can buy back what you made during your time at work (at a profit to your employers, of course); but you can never buy back the *time* you spent at work. That part of your life is gone and you have nothing to show for it but the bills you were able to pay. Eventually

Can you *spend* time, like money?

you start to think of your own creative abilities and labor power as beyond your control, for you come to associate doing anything but "relaxing" (recovering from work) with the misery of doing what you are *told* rather than what you want. The idea of acting on your own initiative and pursuing your own goals no longer occurs to you except when it comes to working on your hobbies.

Yes, there are a few people who find ways to get paid to do exactly what they've always wanted to. But how many of the working people you know fit into that category? These rare, lucky individuals are held up to us as proof that the system works, and we are exhorted to work really, really hard so that one day we can be as lucky as they are, too. The truth is that there are simply not enough job openings for everyone to be a rock star or syndicated cartoonist; somebody has to work in the factories to mass produce the records and newspapers. If you don't succeed in becoming the next world-famous basketball star, and end up selling athletic shoes in a mall instead, you must not have tried hard enough . . . so it's your fault if you're bored there, right? But it wasn't your idea that there should be one thousand shoe salesmen for every professional basketball player. If anything, you can only be blamed for accepting a situation that offers such poor odds. Rather than all competing to be the one at the top of the corporate ladder or the one in a million lottery winner, we should be trying to figure out how to make it possible for *all of us* to do what we want with our lives. For even if you are lucky enough to come out on top, what about the thousands and thousands who didn't make it—the unhappy office clerks, the failed artists, listless grill cooks and fed up hotel maids? Is it in *your* best interest to live in a world filled with people who aren't happy, who never got to chase their dreams . . . who maybe never even got to have dreams?

What does capitalism make people value?

As Jeanette writes in her article on product and process, under capitalism our lives end up revolving around *things*, as if happiness is to be found in possessions rather than in free actions and pursuits. Those who have wealth have it because they spend a lot of time and energy figuring out how to get it from other people. Those who have very little have to spend most of their lives working to get what they need to survive, and all they have as consolation for their lives of hard labor and poverty are the few things they are able to afford to buy— since their *lives* themselves have been bought from them. Between those two social classes are the members of the middle class, who have been bombarded from birth with advertisements and other propaganda proclaiming that happiness, youth, meaning, and everything else in life are to be found in possessions and status symbols. They learn to spend their lives working hard to collect these, rather than taking advantage of whatever chances they might have to seek adventure and pleasure.

Thus capitalism centers everyone's values around what they *have* rather than what they *do*, by making them spend their lives competing for the things they need to survive and achieve social standing. People might be more likely to find happiness in a society that encouraged them to value their ability to act freely and do what they want above all else. To create such a society, we will have to stop competing for control and wealth, and start to share them more freely; only then will everyone be completely free to choose the lives they most want to live, without fear of going hungry or being shut out of society.

They're buying your happiness from you—steal it back!

"But doesn't competition lead to productivity?"

Yes—that's the problem. The competitive "free market" economy not only encourages productivity at all costs, it *enforces* it: for those who do not stay ahead of the competition are trodden under it. And what costs, exactly, are we talking about here? For one thing, there are the long hours we spend at work: forty, fifty, sometimes even sixty hours a week, at the beck and call of bosses and/or customers, working until we're well past exhausted in the race to "get ahead." On top of this, there are the low wages we're paid: most of us aren't paid nearly enough to afford a share of all the things our society has to offer, even though it is our labor that makes them possible. This is because in the competitive market, workers aren't paid what they "deserve" for their labor—they're paid the *smallest* amount their employer can pay without them leaving to look for better wages. That's the "law" of supply and demand. The employer has to do this, because he needs to save as much extra capital as he can for advertising, corporate expansion, and other ways to try to keep ahead of the competition. Otherwise, he might not be an employer for long, and his employees will end up working for a more "competitive" master.

There's a word for those long hours and unfair wages: exploitation. But that's not the only cost of the "productivity" our competitive system encourages. Employers have to cut corners in a thousand other ways, too: that's why our work environments are often unsafe, for example. And if it takes doing things that are ecologically destructive to make money and stay productive, an economic system that rewards productivity above all else gives corporations no reason to resist trampling over wildlife and wilderness to make a buck. That's where our forests went, that's where the ozone layer went, that's where hundreds of species of wild animals went: they were burned up in our rat race. In place of forests, we now have shopping malls and gas stations, not to mention air pollution, because it's more important to have places to buy and sell than it is to preserve environments of peace and beauty. In place of buffalo and bald eagles, we have animals locked in factory farms, turned into milk and meat machines... and singing cartoon animals in Disney movies, the closest thing to wild animals some of us ever see. Our competitive economic system forces us to replace everything free and beautiful with the efficient, the uniform, the profitable.

This isn't limited to our own countries and cultures, of course. Capitalism and its values have spread across the world like a disease.

Competing companies have to keep increasing their markets to keep up with each other, whether by persuasion or by force; that's why you can buy a Coke in Egypt and eat at McDonalds in Thailand. Throughout history we can see examples of how capitalist corporations have forced their way into one country after another, not hesitating to use violence where they deemed it necessary. Today, human beings in almost every corner of the world sell their labor to multinational corporations, often for less than a dollar an hour, in return for the chance to chase the images of wealth and status those corporations use to tantalize them. The wealth that their labor creates is sucked out of their

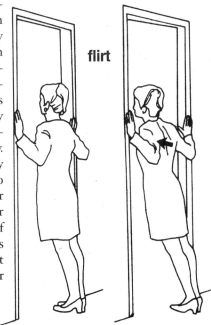

flirt

communities into the pockets of these companies, and in return their unique cultures are replaced by the standard-issue monoculture of Western consumerism. By the same token, people in these countries can hardly afford not to seek to be competitive and "productive" themselves in the same ways that those exploiting them are. Consequently, the whole world is being standardized under one system, the capitalist system . . . and it is getting hard for people to imagine any other way of doing things.

So—what *kind* of productivity does competition encourage? It encourages material productivity alone—that is, profit at any expense. We don't get higher *quality* products, for it is in the manufacturers' best interest that we return to buy from them again when our cars and stereos break down after a few years. We don't get the products that are most relevant to our lives and pursuit of happiness, either: we get the products that are easiest and most profitable to sell. We get credit card companies, telemarketers, junk mail, cigarettes carefully designed to contain eight different addictive chemicals. In order that one company may outsell its competitors, *we* end up spending *our*

Competition means that we don't get to come together and decide what would best for ourselves and the world as a group; nor do we get to decide those things as individuals. Instead, the projects our species undertakes and the changes we make in the world are decided by the laws of competition, by whatever SELLS the most.

lives working to develop, mass-produce, and purchase things like garbage disposal units, conveniences that raise our standard of survival without actually improving our quality of life. Much more than better blenders or video games or potato chips, we need more *meaning* and *pleasure* in our lives, but we're all so busy competing that we don't even have time to think about it.

Surely in a less competitive society, we could still produce all the things we need, without being forced to produce all the frivolous extra stuff that is presently filling up our landfills. And maybe then we could concentrate our efforts on learning how to produce the most important thing of all: human happiness.

So... who *exactly* is it that gets power under capitalism?

In a system where people compete for wealth and the power that comes with it, the ones who are the most ruthless in their pursuit are the ones who end up with the most of both, of course. Thus the capitalist system *encourages* deceit, exploitation, and cutthroat competition, and rewards those who go to those lengths by giving them the most power and the greatest say in what goes on in society.

The corporations who do the best job of convincing us that we need their products, whether we do or not, are the most successful. That's how a company like Coca-Cola, which makes one of the most practically useless products on the market, was able to attain such a position of wealth and power: they were the most successful not at offering something of value to society, but at promoting their product. Coke is not the best tasting beverage the world has ever tasted—

1   **2**   **3**   **play dead**

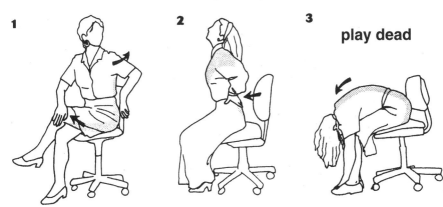

it is simply the most mercilessly marketed. The ones who are most successful at creating an environment that keeps us buying from them, whether that means manipulating us with ad campaigns or using more devious means, are the ones who get the most resources to keep doing what they are doing; and thus, they are the ones who get the most power over the environments we live in. That's why our cities are filled with billboards and corporate skyscrapers, rather than artwork, public gardens, or bathhouses. That's why our newspapers and television programs are filled with slanted perspectives and outright lies: the producers are at the mercy of their advertisers, and the advertisers they depend on most are the ones who have the most money: the ones who are willing to do anything, even twist facts and spread falsehoods, to get and keep that money. (Do a little research and you'll see just how often this happens.) Capitalism virtually guarantees that the ones who control what goes on in society are the greediest, the cruelest, the most heartless.

YOU ARE A TARGET AUDIENCE

Youth is a time when you should be reevaluating the assumptions and traditions of older generations, when you should be willing to set yourself apart from those who have come before and create an identity of your own.

But in our society, "youthful rebellion" has become a ritual: every generation is expected to revolt against the social order for a few years, before "growing up" and "accepting reality." This negates any power for real change that the fresh perspective of youth could have; for now rebellion is "just for kids," and no young person dares to maintain their resistance into adulthood for fear of being thought of as childish.

This arrangement is very much to the advantage of certain corporations who depend on the "youth market." Where is your money going when you buy that compact disc, that chain wallet, that hair dye, leather jacket, wall hanging, all those other accessories that identify you as a rebellious young person? Right to the companies that make up the order you want to stand against. They cash in on your rebellious impulses by selling you symbols of rebellion that actually just keep the wheels turning. You keep their pockets full, and they keep yours empty; they keep you powerless, busy just trying to afford to fit the molds they set for you.

CrimethInc.
"The opium of a new generation."

And since everyone else is at their mercy, and no one wants to end up on the losing side, everyone is encouraged to be greedy, cruel, and heartless. Of course, no one is selfish or hardhearted all the time. Very few people *want* to be, or get much pleasure out of it, and whenever they can avoid it they do. But the average work environment is set up to *make* people cold and impersonal to each other. If somebody comes into a bagel shop starving and penniless, company policy usually requires the employees to send him away empty handed rather than letting anyone have anything without paying—even if the bagel shop throws away dozens of bagels at the end of each day, as most do. The poor employees come to regard the starving people as a nuisance, and the starving people blame the employees for not helping them, when really it is just capitalism pitting them against each other. And, sadly enough, it is probably the employee who enforces ridiculous rules like this the most strictly who will advance to manager.

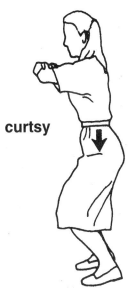

curtsy

Those who dare to spend their lives doing things that are not profitable generally get neither security nor status for their efforts. They may be doing things of great value to society, such as making art or music or doing social work. But if they can't turn a profit from these activities, they will have a hard time surviving, let alone gathering the resources to expand their projects; and, since power comes first and foremost from wealth, they will have little control over what goes on in their society, as well. Thus, corporations that have no goals other than gathering more wealth and power for themselves *always* end up with more power over what goes on in a capitalist society than artists or social activists do. And at the same time, few people can afford to spend much time doing things that are worthwhile but not lucrative. You can imagine what sort of effects this has.

To be rich today is merely to own the largest number of meaningless objects— to possess the greatest amounts of poverty.
–Donald Trump

What kind of place does this make our world?

The capitalist system gives the average person very little control over the collective capabilities and technologies of her society, and very little say in their deployment. Even though it is her labor (and that of people like her) that has made possible the construction of the world she lives in, she feels as though that labor, her own potential and the potential of her fellow human beings, is foreign to her, outside her control, something that acts upon the world regardless of her will. Small wonder if she feels frustrated, powerless, unfulfilled, dreamless. But it is not just this lack of control that makes capitalism so hostile to human happiness. In place of democratic control over our lives and our society, we have the heartless dominion of force.

Violence is not only present when human beings do physical harm to each other. Violence is there, albeit in a subtler form, whenever they use force upon each other in their interactions. It is violence that is at the root of capitalism. Under the capitalist system, all the

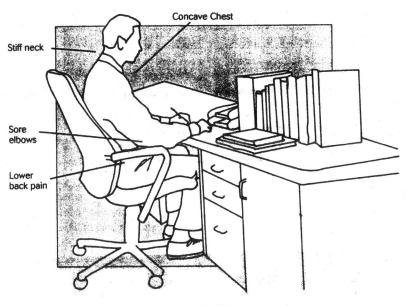

Stiff neck

Concave Chest

Sore elbows

Lower back pain

A typical desk setup

economic laws governing human life come down to coercion: *Work or go hungry! Dominate or be dominated! Compete or perish! Sell the hours of your life away for the means to survive, or rot in poverty—or jail!*

Most people go to work because they *have* to, not because they want to. They sell their time to buy food and shelter, and to pay the bills for all the status symbols and luxuries they have been conditioned to collect, only because they know that the alternative is starvation and ostracism. They may like some of the things they do at their jobs, but they would much rather do these things on their own time and in their own way—and do other things, besides, that their jobs leave them no time or energy for. To force the maximum productivity out of people who would rather be elsewhere, corporations use a thousand mechanisms of control: they schedule work hours for their employees, make them punch timeclocks, keep them under constant observation. Bosses and workers are brought together under mutual economic duress, and they negotiate with each other under invisible threats: the one pointing the gun of unemployment and poverty to the other's head, the other threatening poor service and, possibly, strikes. Most people try to maintain some concern for the human needs of others, even on the job; but the essence of our economy is competition and domination, and that always comes out in our relationships with those above and below us in the work hierarchy.

Can you imagine how much more advantageous, and how much more *fun,* it could be for all of us if we were able to act out of love, rather than compulsion? If we did things for the sheer joy of doing them, and worked together because we *wanted* to, not because we had to? Wouldn't that make it more enjoyable to do the things that are necessary for survival—and to be around each other, for that matter?

For these patterns of violence inevitably spill over into the rest of our lives, too. When you're used to regarding people as objects, as resources to be spent or enemies to be feared and fought, it's hard to leave those values behind you when you come home. The hierarchy that private ownership imposes upon relationships in the workplace can be found everywhere else in society: in schools, in churches, in families and in friendships, everywhere the dynamics of domination and submission take place. It's almost impossible to imagine what a truly equal relationship could consist of, in a society where everyone is always jockeying for superiority. When children fight in grade school or rival gangs war in the streets, they are merely imitating the greater conflicts that take place between and within corporations and the

Without our chewing gum, no one will want to kiss you. Without our deodorant, no one will want to touch you. Without our lipstick, you won't catch anyone's eye. Without our athletic shoes, you won't be able to keep up with the guys. Without our cigarettes, sophistication escapes you. Without our cleaning products, no one will want to come home to you. Your children won't have any games to play without our toys and cartoons. She won't enjoy the date unless you take her to see one of our movies. The fun hasn't really started until you have our beer in your hand. How can you feel free and alive without our new sports car?

Consider all your leisure-time activities and you'll see: you're not having fun unless you're paying for it.

We play on your insecurities, on your fears and anxieties. There are products for every human activity, even sex, because the things that are *natural* and *free* are not good enough without our synthetic supplements. Eventually you're so conditioned that you'll pay for the most useless of products, just to be paying for something. And should you ever try to step outside our system, you'll see that we really have made it impossible to be a human being without our products: you must pay to eat, pay to sleep, pay to keep warm, pay for a space just to *exist*.

CrimethInc.
"Depend on us!"

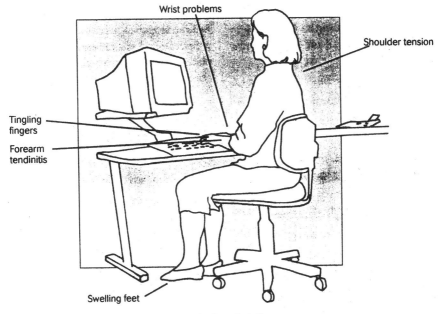

A typical workstation

nations that serve their interests; their violence is regarded as an anomaly, but it is just a reflection of the violent, competitive world that fostered them. When potential friends or lovers evaluate each other in terms of financial worth and status rather than according to heart and soul, they are simply acting out the lessons they have been taught about "market value"—living under the reign of force, it's almost impossible not to look at other human beings and the world in general in terms of what's in it for you.

If we lived in a world where we could pursue whatever aspirations we pleased, without fear of dying hungry, crazy, and unloved like Van Gogh and a thousand others, our lives and relationships would no longer be molded by violence. Perhaps then it would be easier for us to look at each other and see what is beautiful and unique, to look at nature and appreciate it for what it is . . . to be and let be rather than always seeking power and advantage. There have been hundreds of other societies in the history of our species in which people have lived that way. Is it really too much to think that we could reorganize our own society to be more democratic?

OK, OK, but what's the alternative?

The alternative to capitalism would be a consensual society in which we could decide individually (and, where necessary, collectively) what our lives and surroundings would be, instead of being forced into them by so-called laws like "supply and demand." Those are only laws if we let them be. It's hard to imagine a society based on cooperation from this vantage point, since the only societies most of us have seen in our lives are based on competition. But such societies are possible: they have existed over and over in the history of our species, and they can exist again, if we want.

To escape from the fetters of competition, we need to develop an economy that is based on giving rather than trading: a *gift* economy, in place of this exchange economy. In such a system, each person could do what she wanted to with her life, and offer to others what she felt most qualified to offer, without fear of going hungry. The means to do things would be shared by everyone rather than hoarded up by the

greediest individuals, so each person would have all the capabilities of society at her disposal. Those who wanted to paint could paint, those who enjoy building engines and machines could do that, those who love bicycles could make and repair them for others. The so-called "dirty work" would be spread around more fairly, and everyone would benefit from being able to do a variety of things rather than being limited to one trade like a cog in a machine. "Work" itself would be a thousand times more pleasurable, without tight schedules or demanding bosses constraining us. And though we might have a slower rate of production, we would have a wider array of creative pursuits in our society, which could make life fuller and more meaningful for all of us . . . besides, do we really need all the trinkets and luxuries we slave so hard to make today?

This sounds like an utopian vision, and it is, but that doesn't mean that we can't make our lives a lot more like that than they are

"He had learned the way of things about him now. It was a war of each against all, and the devil take the hindmost. You did not give feasts to other people, you waited for them to give feasts to you. You went about with your soul full of suspicion and hatred; you understood that you were environed by hostile powers that were trying to get your money, and who used all the virtues to bait their traps with. The storekeepers plastered up their windows with all sorts of lies to entice you; the very fences by the wayside, the lampposts and telephone poles, were pasted over with lies. The great corporation which employed you lied to you, and lied to the whole country—from top to bottom it was nothing but one gigantic lie."
–Walt Whitman, *The Jungle*

now. We don't have to look only to the bushmen of the Kalahari desert for examples of what life is like outside capitalism, either: even today, there are plenty of opportunities in our own society to see how much better life is when nothing has a price. Whenever a knitting circle meets to share friendship and advice, whenever people go camping together and divide up responsibilities, whenever people cooperate to cook or make music or do anything else for pleasure rather than money, that is the "gift economy" in action. One of the most exhilarating things about being in love or having a close friend is that, for once, you are valued for who you are, not what you're "worth." And what a wonderful feeling it is to enjoy things in life that come to you free, without having to measure how much of yourself you are exchanging for them! Even in this society, almost everything we derive real pleasure from comes from outside the confines of capitalist relations. And why shouldn't we demand *all* the time what works so well in our private lives? If we get so much more out of our relationships when they are free from the coercion of ownership and competition, why shouldn't we seek to free our "work relationships" from that coercion as well?

But who will collect the garbage, if we all do what we want? Well, when a group of friends live in an apartment together, doesn't the garbage get taken out? It might not get taken out as regularly as it would by the janitor at an office, but it gets taken out *voluntarily,* and it isn't always the same guy stuck doing it. To suggest that we can't provide for our own needs without authority forcing us to is to vastly underestimate and insult our species. The idea that we would all sit around doing nothing if we didn't have to work for bosses to survive comes

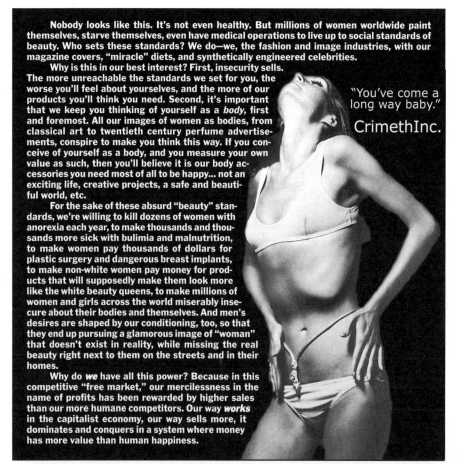

Nobody looks like this. It's not even healthy. But millions of women worldwide paint themselves, starve themselves, even have medical operations to live up to social standards of beauty. Who sets these standards? We do—we, the fashion and image industries, with our magazine covers, "miracle" diets, and synthetically engineered celebrities.

Why is this in our best interest? First, insecurity sells. The more unreachable the standards we set for you, the worse you'll feel about yourselves, and the more of our products you'll think you need. Second, it's important that we keep you thinking of yourself as a *body*, first and foremost. All our images of women as bodies, from classical art to twentieth century perfume advertisements, conspire to make you think this way. If you conceive of yourself as a body, and you measure your own value as such, then you'll believe it is our body accessories you need most of all to be happy... not an exciting life, creative projects, a safe and beautiful world, etc.

For the sake of these absurd "beauty" standards, we're willing to kill dozens of women with anorexia each year, to make thousands and thousands more sick with bulimia and malnutrition, to make women pay thousands of dollars for plastic surgery and dangerous breast implants, to make non-white women pay money for products that will supposedly make them look more like the white beauty queens, to make millions of women and girls across the world miserably insecure about their bodies and themselves. And men's desires are shaped by our conditioning, too, so that they end up pursuing a glamorous image of "woman" that doesn't exist in reality, while missing the real beauty right next to them on the streets and in their homes.

Why do *we* have all this power? Because in this competitive "free market," our mercilessness in the name of profits has been rewarded by higher sales than our more humane competitors. Our way *works* in the capitalist economy, our way sells more, it dominates and conquers in a system where money has more value than human happiness.

"You've come a long way baby."

CrimethInc.

from the fact that, since we *do* have to work for bosses to survive, we would all rather sit around doing nothing. But if we had our energy and our time to ourselves, we would rediscover how to use them, for practical purposes as well as impractical: remember how many people enjoy gardening for its own sake, even when they don't have to do it to survive. Surely we wouldn't let ourselves starve to death in a society where we shared decisions and power rather than fighting over them . . . and the fact that so many people are starving *today* indicates that capitalism is no less impractical than any other system might be.

We're often told it is "human nature" to be greedy, and that this is why our world is the way it is. The very existence of other societies and other ways of life contradicts this. Once you realize that modern capitalist society is only one of a thousand ways that human beings have lived and interacted together, you can see that this talk of "human nature" is nonsense. We are formed first and foremost by the environments we grow up in—and human beings now have the power to construct our own environments. If we are ambitious enough, we can design our world to reconstruct us in any shape our hearts desire. Yes, all of us are haunted by feelings of greed and aggression, living as we do in a materialistic and violent world. But in more supportive environments, built on different values, we could learn to interact in ways that would bring more pleasure to all of us. Indeed, most of us would be far more generous and considerate today if we could be—it's hard to give gifts freely in a world where you have to sell a part of yourself away in order to get anything at all. Considering that, it's amazing how many gifts we still give each other.

The people who talk about "human nature" would tell us that this nature consists chiefly of the lust to possess and control. But what about our desires to share, and to act for the sheer sake of acting? Only those who have given up on *doing* what they want content themselves by finding meaning in what they merely have. Almost everyone knows that it is more rewarding to bring joy to others than it is to take things from them. Acting freely and giving freely are their own reward. Those who think that "from each according to her means, to each according to her needs" unfairly benefits the receivers have simply misunderstood what makes human beings happy.

It's tempting to think of capitalism as a conspiracy of the rich against everyone else, and to conceive of the struggle against capitalism as a struggle against them. But in truth, it is in *everyone's* best interest that we do away with this economic system. If true wealth consists of freedom and community, we are all poor here: for even to be "rich" in a society that is hostile to those things is only to possess

(continued from page 80)

The alienation, distrust and exhaustion we all feel in this society multiply our needs, and we run to commodities (invested with fetishistic power as they are by advertisements) hoping they can save us. But purchasing them only perpetuates our misery. For every time you buy something in this system, you're buying the whole system: you're giving your money to the corporations to reinforce their power, and to get that money, you have to give your labor to them too. That's more labor for them to maintain "business as usual," and less freedom for you to fight back!

I've resolved to get the fuck out any way that I can. I'm going to stop working for them, stop paying for all their products, stop believing in all the myths about having the perfect home and the perfect car and "getting ahead" in the (aptly named) "work force." I'm going to create a life for myself that I want to live, that I can find joy in, or die trying. But even if I do escape, how can I live the life I yearn for if all the people I care about, all the people around me and the world I live in itself, remain under the power of this system? It will be just as lonely being free if everyone else is still locked inside the schools and offices and factories, following instructions. If I want to truly get out of here, I have to figure out how to take the others with me. I walk down the street, watching smog pour into the sky from smokestacks, and I ache for a world in which it is up to us whether the stacks ever smoke again.

And where are the pleasure gardens that could have been built with all this labor, or the woods to wander through, the rivers to drink from, the lakes to swim in? Where are the eagles and moose to admire, or the stars in the light- and air-polluted night sky, for that matter? In my daydreams, I travel through beautiful wilderlands, meeting people who have unique customs and ways of life, who never heard of Pepsi, who never spent a day doing anything but what they please. Together we concoct wild schemes of how to wrest the most pleasure out of life, how to squeeze it to the very last drop . . . and we roll all our desires and fantasies together into one great ball, with which to smash open the gates to paradise itself.

the greatest amounts of poverty. This system is not the result of an evil plot by a few villains bent on world domination—and even if it was, they've only succeeded in condemning everyone, themselves included, to the shackles of domination and submission. Let's not be too jealous of them just because they seem better off from a distance. Anyone who has grown up in one of their households can tell you that for all their bank accounts and sprinkler systems, they're no happier or freer than you are. We should try to find ways to make *everyone* see what is to be gained from transforming our society, and to involve everyone in it.

If that's a difficult challenge, and it sometimes seems to you that "the masses" deserve what they get for accepting this way of life, don't lose heart. Remember, the system *they* accept is the one *you* live under. Your chances for liberation are inextricably tied to theirs.

Don't be paralyzed by the seeming vastness of the forces arranged against us—those work forces are made up of people just like you, yearning to break free. Find ways to escape from the system of violence in your own life, and take them with you when you can. Seize any free moment, any opportunity you can get your hands on; life can be sold away, but it can't be bought—only stolen back!

"TELEVISION SUCKS, DUDE."

So, you've become dubious, cynical? You don't trust the government, Coca-Cola, television anymore? We're perfectly happy to parody ourselves, to insult ourselves, even to explain all of our ugly intentions and evil dealings in detail... as long as it keeps your attention. We have television shows, advertisements, and comic strips carefully designed for those of you who don't have confidence in us anymore. Anything to keep you *watching*, anything to keep you *buying*.

We play on your cynicism, cashing in on it, encouraging it. You may know better than to have any faith in us, but as long as we keep you captivated with our irony and self-deprecation, you won't be able to conceive of any alternatives. Rather than having the idealism to strike out against the status quo, you'll join the ranks of the *Dilbert* nihilists, no longer able to believe in anything, but still playing your part in the system of despair.

CrimethInc.
(you are a captive audience)

(continued from page 82)

of the work week until the moment I cash my paycheck weeks later, they get an interest-free loan in the form of my labor. And the landlord gets the same loan from me when I pay a month ahead for my lodgings—not to mention the government, which takes taxes out of my paycheck for a whole year in advance! In the meantime, I have to be careful not to turn the heat up higher than I can afford, or eat more food than I can afford, or talk to my faraway friends on the phone longer than I can afford . . . and when I'm shivering, and my stomach is growling, and I feel lonely, I can't help but be furious that, though technologies are in place that could easily keep me as warm and well-fed as could be, I have to pay dearly for every crumb—so a few rich men can gather more wealth at my expense! I work forty hours a week for the system that makes all these amenities possible—do I not *deserve* to turn the heat up as high as my boss can, just because I get dirtier on the job? Do I not *deserve* to taste the food at the restaurants he frequents, just because I don't want to fight my way up the corporate ladder?

It's much worse for some of my friends: they have credit card bills and loans to pay off. Those corporations have control over them for life: no matter what they may want to do, next month or ten years from now, they will be at their mercy. That's a few extra hundred dollars a month most of them have to raise, and that means unless they're willing to declare bankruptcy they'll never be free of the compulsion to sell their lives away. It enrages me every time I receive another promotional credit card application in the mail, knowing that these motherfuckers will do anything to suck me in, to trap me in the indentured servitude of debt. And I wince whenever I see my friends buying more stuff, in empty attempts to console themselves: of course they're desperate for freedom and excitement, living the lives that they do, but they're not going to find any of those things in a stereo or a new Jeep! Spending their money like that just keeps them chained tighter to the system that is stealing their lives from them. Some of them spend the whole year working, their hearts silent within their chests, to save up the money for a few weeks and weekends of hiking, skiing, canoeing—things that were once free for all of us, before the corporations we work for wrapped everything in concrete.

Postscript: A Class War *Everyone* Can Fight In

The poverty against which man has been struggling throughout history is not merely the poverty of material goods; the ennui and disorientation experienced by the members of the middle and upper classes in today's wealthy industrial nations have revealed the poverty of Western existench itself.

The problems that we face today cannot be traced to class conflict alone. It is not merely a question of the ruling class profiting at the expense of the proletariat, for we have seen that the profit that those with capital do make does not make their lives any more fulfilling. It does not matter whether a woman is buried alive in a prison, in a reform school, in a sweatshop, in a ghetto, in a prestigious university, in a condominium bought on credit, or in a mansion with a private swimming pool and tennis courts, so long as she is buried alive. Everyone suffers from today's status quo, albeit differently; but whether a man is starving on his minimum wage salary, exhausted by his repetitive responsibilities at the office, or befuddled by the feeling of emptiness that accompanies the undirected acquisition of material wealth, he has a stake in fighting for change. So we all, rich and poor, must band together to transform our situation.

This also means that there is no mythical "They." Innumerable radical movements and social critics have relied upon this concept to motivate people by stirring up hatred for the "evil orchestrators" of human suffering, the enemies who conspire against us. But this kind of thinking only serves to divide us against each other, and whether we are divided on class lines, on color lines, or according to other categories, we are distracted from the important issues and impeded in our progress. Our true "enemy" is the social forces and patterns at work between us, and it is these forces which we must come to understand and to struggle against.

This is not to say that there are not individuals whose behavior is particularly dangerous to their fellow human beings, insofar as it perpetuates and intensifies our present state of emergency. But even if these individuals do have negative intentions towards others, it is still unlikely that they possess a clear understanding of the extremely complicated conditions to which they are contributing. Our social and economic relations are snarled and harmful in such complex ways that no secret society of evil geniuses could ever have arranged this fate for us.

And let no one say these individuals say are benefiting at the expense of the rest of us. If gaining material wealth and status in a murderous society really is benefiting, then we should just let things stay the way they are and put our energy into fighting each against all to get to the top of the dungheap. If these people's lives are not as impoverished as our own, our whole value system is bankrupt. It's understandable that some of us are jealous of their disproportionate control over the resources of our society . . . but it's not having stuff or status that makes life good, is it?

Enough abstractions! Let's talk about real life!

actual testimony by a real life member of the working proletariat!

How does it feel to never be treated like an adult? To never be free of rules and regulations put upon you "for your own good," to have to obey and grovel before teachers, bosses, policemen—because they serve masters who have more money and power over *your* life than you can ever hope to achieve? To have to beg and scheme and lie for an afternoon "off" to do what you want, for once? To answer to automated bells, to be at the mercy of machines and clocks and people with half your brains and personality, to be dressed in matching uniforms like identical bags of potato chips? To be required to recite standard phrases over and over all day—to be programmed like a machine?

Do you think it's really a coincidence that Coca-Cola is now sold on every corner of the earth's? Do you really trust them to have all that power, to make this planet a place you want to live?

Every time I get home to find my mailbox filled with junk mail, every time I try to eat a quiet dinner with one of my lovers and we get interrupted by a phone call from a telemarketing company, I'm reminded that I live in a society that values sales more than privacy. Every time someone has a television on and a barrage of commercials assaults us, I remember how little truth and quiet reflection matter to the merchants out to make a "killing." Every time I ride my bike, I pass billboards proclaiming the power and sex appeal of various trivial products, and it infuriates me to imagine all the better uses that public space could have been put to. If only there was a way for us to decide what goes up on our own streets, besides writing graffiti!

And when bills come due, I'm reminded again of what counts in this golden age. I have to pay the rent at the beginning of the month, *before* I've stayed in the apartment for one night, but I don't get paid until at least three weeks *after* my work week begins—because the people who control the property I live on, and the workplace I have to serve in, have slanted everything in their favor. From the beginning

---

5 At the time of this writing, in some Latin American nations Coca Cola is responsible for the sales of over 60% of drinkable liquids *of any kind.* According-ing to their five year report, their next objective is to make Coke machines more common than *water fountains.* Don't they realize they're just a soft drink company? The human body is over 90% water... how much of your body have you *purchased* from Coca Cola? How about from other corporations? They say you are what you eat . . .

THE PARIS COMMUNE

Thanks to a popular uprising, Paris was transformed into a sort of continuous anarchist festival for a few months, before the usual spoilsports regained control and slaughtered everybody. ❋

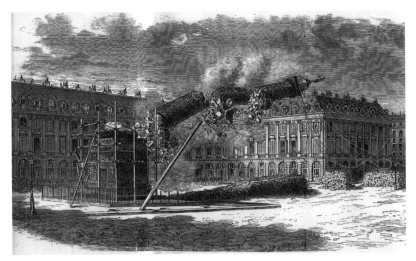

CLIMB ABOARD THE DRUNKEN BOAT ON PAGE 92

*"Culture? Uh! That's the commodity they want us to buy most of all—
the one that makes us think we need all the others."*
–Marilyn Monroe, in her suicide note

"When I hear the word culture, I reach for my wallet."
–Ayn Rand, explaining how she set about climbing the social ladder

From Over-the-Counter-Culture to Beneath the Underground.

The problem of culture was first addressed over eight decades ago in the dada journal *Icarus Was Right*:

"Culture: a) the customary beliefs, social forms, and material traits of a racial, religious, or social group. b) the set of shared attitudes, values, goals and practices that characterizes a defined group.

"Hopefully it is obvious after reading the above definition that culture, any culture, is inherently evil and problematic. Who wants to have to conform, and force others to conform, to the predefined beliefs and values of a "racial, religious, or social group"?"

What the author was working on in this article was a critique of the way traditions shape our lives. "Culture" of any kind is made up of traditions, of patterns of action and interaction passed along from one person to the next. That is to say: culture itself consists of prescribed limitations upon the actions, interactions, and even thoughts of human beings. These limitations can be beneficial—for example, when they contain useful information for accomplishing practical tasks such as cooking—but they can also limit human beings in dangerous ways. Culture can be as benign as traditional Italian cuisine and as loathsome as the sexism and racism that is a fundamental part of many societies. So it's easy to see how "culture," by this definition, could be hostile to human happiness.

But culture is *always* a dangerous phenomenon, not just when it teaches people sexism and racism—because while every culture teaches certain values and ways of doing things, prescribing them as if they

are right for everyone, human beings are all different and have different needs. Any given culture may be right for some people at some point in their lives, but no culture is right for everyone—and, since people change, there is no guarantee that a particular culture will be right for a person for her entire life. Of course it is impossible to eradicate culture from our lives. The idea itself is ridiculous—everything we are is a result of culture: without it, we wouldn't even have language, wouldn't be able to think about the world in the ways that we do. Besides, there are plenty of good things besides language and advanced tool-use that we could not have without the existence of culture: art movements, good cooking, literature, to name a few. The solution, instead, is to be wary of culture and tradition: never to accept them as given but rather to choose what is right for you at the time and reject the rest. Keep a clear awareness of how your behavior, attitudes, and ideas are shaped by the culture or cultures around you. Perhaps you enjoy the more laid-back and romantic approach to life that is a part of Spanish culture, but you find their attitudes towards women despicable; or perhaps you appreciate the passionate music and social criticism of punk "culture" but find that the dancing and funny clothing styles do nothing for you. Take what works for you and leave the rest—then there will be no danger that you will be led astray by any of them. To quote Robin Hood: "The supermarket of ideas, like any supermarket, is fit only for looting."

Today, when the United States, given world domination by its economic power, bulldozes over other cultures and replaces them with its own, there are many groups who oppose this angrily. They demand the freedom to retain their "own" culture and fight to protect it in the face of the encroachment of others. In doing this, they are fighting for the right to be restrained by their own traditions and customs; but they should fight for the right to be restrained by *no* traditions and customs, to invent their ways of living and thinking according to their own needs and desires, and only take ideas and customs from any culture when those ideas and customs happen to be right for them. Culture has the capacity to play a positive, useful role in our lives, but first we must escape from its tyranny over us, which we have granted it with our blind acceptance of its constraints.

is for Death
and Domestication

The Concealment of Death

"Because we don't know when we will die, we get to think of life as an inexhaustible well. But everything happens only a certain number of times, and a very small number, really. How many more times will you remember a certain afternoon of your childhood, some afternoon that is so deeply a part of your being that you can't even conceive of your life without it? Perhaps four or five times more, perhaps not even that. How many more times will you watch the full moon rise? Perhaps twenty. And yet it all seems limitless."
—Gloria Cubana, The Sheltering Sky

Here's an exercise to try at home. You will need a working stopwatch, or another timepiece that measures seconds. Before you begin, seat yourself in a comfortable chair and loosen your clothing. *Watch the second hand as it passes around the face of the clock. Picture the moment of your death, perhaps many decades in the future, or perhaps only a few years or months (who can know?). Wait for the second hand to reach the starting point at the top of the clockface, and then watch as it records the passing of one minute of your life. Now imagine the clock counting down the minutes of your life to the moment of your death. Try this exercise picturing this moment a few decades in the future, then repeat it picturing the moment next year. Repeat it picturing the moment of your death next month. Next week. Tonight. After all, you never know.*

Now observe the minute and hour hands on the clock. What were you doing at this time twenty four hours ago? Forty eight hours ago? One month ago? What will you be doing at this time next week?

Imagine that the moment of your death is one month away. Consider—if you knew that this was true, what would you be doing right now? What would you be doing at this time tomorrow? Repeat this step, imagining your death to be one year away. Does this make very much difference in your thoughts about what you would do today and tomorrow if you knew the date of your death?

Compare your activities over the last twenty four hours to the activities you would have chosen if you had known that you would leave this world in one month or one year. Compare your activities over the last month, the last year, the last decade to those you would have chosen if you had known that on this day you would have only thirty days or twelve months left to live. How different would your life have been if you had known the date of your approaching death? Would you be ready to die in a month or a year, having lived the life that you have?

Chances are, at least as far as we all know, that most of the people who read this text and participate in this exercise will live for many more years afterwards. But still, look at the second hand of the stopwatch, and follow it as it records the passing minutes, counting down the minutes of your life that remain to you as they slip away. Are you living the life that you want to live? Are you living a life that, at any given moment, you could look back upon with satisfaction if you suddenly realized that it was about to end? Are you living the sort of life that you would wish upon a human being, a life that is exciting and full, that is well spent, every minute of it? If the answer is no, what can you do in the time that still remains to you—however long or short that may be— to make your life more like the one you would like to live? For we all do have only a limited amount of time granted to us in this world—we should use it with this in mind.

If you find, looking back upon your life, that you have spent years living without any consideration of your mortality, this is really not unusual, for our social/cultural environment does not encourage us to think much about the limits that nature places on our lives. Death and aging are denied and hidden away as if they were shameful and embarrassing. The older members of our society are hidden away in "retirement homes" like lepers in leper colonies. The billboards, magazine photos, and television commercials that meet our eyes at every turn show only images of healthy men and women in the prime of their life. Cemeteries, which once memorialized the dead and preserved a place for them in the thoughts of the living, are now forgotten in abandoned neighborhoods and overgrown with weeds. When a man dies, the rituals which once would have celebrated his life and brought the subject of human mortality to the thoughts of those who survived him are now often regarded as mere inconveniences. Death is impolite and embarrassing, it is considered bad etiquette—there is no time for it in today's busy world of corporate mergers and record-breaking conspicuous consumption. Our busy schedules and glossy magazines neither make allowance for it nor offer any explanation of how it might be relevant to our value system or our lives.

And indeed if we were to stop and ponder the subject, perhaps we would find that when we seriously consider the limits of our time on this planet, keeping up with television comedies and having a good résumé seem less important than they did before. Our cultural silence about human mortality allows us to forget how much weight the individual moments of our lives carry, adding up as they do to our lives themselves. Thus we squander countless hours watching television or balancing checkbooks—hours that in retrospect we might have done better to have spent walking on the seashore with our loved ones, cooking gourmet meals for our children or friends, writing fiction, or hitchhiking across South America. The reality of our future death is not easy for any of us to come to terms with, but it is surely better that we consider this now than regret not doing so when it is too late.

Our denial of death has a deeper significance, beyond its functions as a reaction to our fear of mortality and a selective blindness that helps preserve the status quo. It is a symptom of our ongoing struggle to escape from the cycles of change in nature and establish an unnatural permanence in the world. Our mortality is frightening evidence that we do not have control over everything: thus we are quick to ignore it, if we cannot do away with it altogether—a feat towards which our medical researchers are working at breakneck speed. It is worth questioning whether this would even be desirable.

Since the dawn of Western civilization, men and women have hungered for domination not only of the world and each other, but also for domination of the seasons, of time itself. We speak of the eternal grandeur of our gods and empires, and we design our cities and corporations to exist into infinity. We build monuments, skyscrapers, which we intend to stand forever as testimony of our victory over the sands of time. But this victory can only come at a price, at this price: that though nothing passes away, nothing comes to be, either—that the world we create is a static, standardized place that can hold no surprises for us any more. We would do well to be wary of fulfilling our own darkest dreams by creating such a dystopia, a frozen world in which no one must fear death any more, for everyone exists forever and no one lives for even an instant.

Alive in the land of the dead. They eat dead food with false teeth. Their buildings have false fronts, their radio and television stations broadcast dead air. They kill time as spectators of false images. Their corporations are guilty of false advertising, and their employment 'opportunities' offer only murderous mistreatment, lethal boredom, and fatal submission; they demand that you meet deadlines, that you pitch tent in the death camps. Does the dead end justify the means? They inhabit dead cities and make false moves, really going nowhere at all, treading day after day the same path of despair. Even their air is conditioned. They ask you to give your lives for their countries, for their religions, for their economies, leaving you with only . . . . Their system is organized by artificial intelligence and provides only virtual reality. Their culture will pin you down and bore you to death, their lifestyle is lifeless, their existench is a permanent deadlock. Everything about them is dead and false. The only thing that is unbearable is that *nothing* is unbearable. When will we demand more?

The struggle is for **life**, for **real** life. Fight foul, life is real!

RIMBAUD'S DEATHBED CONVERSION

Arthur Rimbaud converted on his deathbed to the Christianity he once despised—setting a new precedent for living life to the fullest.

Rimbaud was born as the second of four children to a farmer's daughter living in rural France. At the age of sixteen, he ran away to live homeless on the streets of Paris, writing poetry that was at once visionary and blasphemous. He made the acquaintance of the poet Verlaine, with whom he stayed until Verlaine's wife forced him to leave; Verlaine had fallen in love with him, and continued to support him, despite the scandal their homosexual relationship caused. Rimbaud wreaked havoc throughout Paris, knocking the hats off priests in the street, verbally and physically assaulting the popular poets Verlaine introduced him to, and destroying Verlaine's marriage. The two ran away into the countryside together, then moved to London to live in abject poverty until Rimbaud, disgusted with Verlaine, who claimed he couldn't live without him, decided to leave.

In desperation, Verlaine shot Rimbaud, wounding him in the wrist. The police came and Verlaine was jailed for two years, on charges not of assault but sodomy; meanwhile Rimbaud escaped to his mother's farm,

"Life is elsewhere." – young Arthur in his journals, one month before leaving his mother's farm for the first time.

where he completed the body of poems that was to change poetry and writing itself forever. Then, at the age of eighteen, Rimbaud put down his pen and announced he was done with being a poet. He learned four more languages (German, Arabic, Russian, and Hindustani—he already knew French, English, and Latin, among others) and set off traveling: he crossed the Alps on foot, joined the Dutch colonial army and deserted in the Indies, joined a German circus touring Scandinavia, visited Egypt, and worked as a laborer in Cyprus. Throughout all these adventures, he was plagued by serious illnesses and health problems, but he never let them slow him down. At the age of twenty nine, he became the first white man to journey to the Ogaden region of Ethiopia, and his report (published in the proceedings of the Geographical Society) aroused interest in academic circles.

Rimbaud soon moved to Ethiopia as a gun runner, and became close with the people there, living with a native woman and befriending the Ethiopian king. He received a letter from a famous poetry magazine in France, begging him to return to lead the new literary movement that had grown up around his writings, but didn't even bother to answer it. He didn't return to

Europe until he developed a tumor in his right knee, which forced him to travel, borne on a stretcher, the thousands of miles back to France. There, his leg was amputated, and he languished in the care of his Christian mother and sister until, at the edge of death, exhausted beyond the bounds of even his love of life and truth, he made confession to a priest—before expiring at the age of thirty-six.

Rimbaud knew better than to save any of himself for the grave: he spent every resource he had in this world down to the last penny—burned money, health, friends, family, sanity as so much fuel for the fire—so when Death came to take him away He got nothing, not even a man with his pride or common sense intact. His life still stands as an example to us all. 🏵

TOWARDS THE ENDS OF THE EARTH ON PAGE 99

"Arnold Schwarznegger was factory farmed. We're free range."
–Paul F. Maul Artists' Group worker F. Markatos Dixon,
on the subject of an art/terrorism intervention he performed
at a body building gym

THE DOMESTICATION OF ANIMALS . . .
. . . AND OF MAN.

Perhaps you wonder sometimes if we're getting carried away with our criticism of modern day life, if all the talk about the evil system and our sick society is just youthful rebelliousness and exaggeration. It certainly is hard to tell from here inside the human race, with all our dissembling and projecting and pretense, whether what we're do-ing really makes sense or not . . . so who knows, maybe things aren't so fucked up, right? If you want some perspective on whether the brave new world order really is as bad for us as some people say, just have a look at how it affects the others who must live in it—the animals.

If you're middle class, the animals you know best (besides the ones in animated movies and commercials) are probably the ones who occupy the corresponding tier of the non-human hierarchy: the house-hold pets, the zoo inmates and circus performers, the sports mascots and show horses. Just like the bourgeoisie, they seem to have it easy: sitting around all day, eating and sleeping, playing with their masters— but this is not the life these animals have been prepared for over the last million years of evolution. Dogs have four legs so they can run through fields and canyons and chase down prey, not play frisbee for an hour a week. Parrots have wings so they can fly over jungles and across wild landscapes, not just sit, wings cut away, in little cages, with nothing to do to maintain their spirits but sing to themselves and learn meaningless fragments of less musical languages. Cats have claws so they can fight and hunt and sharpen them anywhere they choose, they have testicles and ovaries so they can mark territory and go into heat and make love and raise kittens; cut all these off and keep them locked inside, and they get grouchy, pathetic, fat for lack of anything to do but eat standard-issue canned food they can't even hunt. Domestic animals are expected to be the court jesters and courtesans of the modern household, to provide entertainment and surrogate community, and their lives and even bodies are adjusted accordingly. Their role is not to *be animals,* in all the wondrous complexity that entails, but simply to be toys.

A quick look back at middle class humans reveals how similar our situation is. We too live in isolation from our fellows in small, climate-controlled boxes, little fishtanks complete with simulated foliage, called apartments. We too are fed on standardized, mass-produced food that appears as if out of nowhere, vastly different from the food our ancestors ate. We too have no outlet for our wild, spontaneous urges, sterilized and declawed by the necessities of living in cramped cities and suburbs under cramping legal and social and cultural conventions. We too cannot wander far from our kennels, leashed as we are by 9-to-5 jobs, apartment leases, fences and property lines

and national borders. And just like our pets, we learn to behave, to be housebroken and spirit-broken—to adapt ourselves to this nightmare, becoming fat, grouchy, songless.

Far less fortunate than us castrated prisoners, animal and human alike, are the animals that form the non-human proletariat: the chickens trapped living in their own shit in egg-factories with their beaks removed so they won't peck out each others' eyes, the rabbits that have their eyes systematically burned out to test the safety of shampoo, the veal calves that spend their entire miserable existences in tiny wooden boxes. The roles these animals play correspond to those of factory workers, temporary dishwashers and secretaries, minimum-waged movie theater popcorn servers—and however individual bosses might see things, you can bet the market views them all with the same calculating disinterest. The same profit-hungry heartlessness that makes it possible for the meat industry to regard the yearly holocaust of millions of animals as fine and just keeps them doing their best to fight off demands for better working conditions and higher wages. And just as cows and chickens have been carefully bred, even genetically engineered, to such an extent that they are unable to survive outside their cages, the modern worker no longer has any concept of what life outside the working world of plastic and concrete might be, or how to apply his energies except under a whip. Where would he go, anyway, were he to escape? Are there habitable lands as yet unclaimed, to which he could flee? And wouldn't he destroy these lands, too, bringing to them the values of domination with which he has been poisoned by his bosses? In the end, unless advised by a total rejection of industrial capitalism, his flight would be just another advance in the tide of concrete that is sweeping across the globe.

Finally, there are the wild animals which still survive in environments polluted with oil slicks, discarded plastic soda bottles, and air pollution, to say nothing of highways and hunters. As urbanization and suburbanization march pitilessly forward, destroying the resources of their natural habitats, they learn to live off human waste instead, or perish. Pigeons build nests out of cigarette butts instead of twigs, rats learn to live in sewers and adapt accordingly, cockroaches proliferate as the vultures of the new era. These urban wild animals occupy the same tier of society as the homeless do, scrounging through the refuse for the bare essentials of life, although they certainly fare better than their human counterparts. The suburban ones—the wily raccoons, possums, squirrels who survive in the forgotten corners of conquered lands, living off what's left of the natural, not to mention the extras and excesses of the bourgeoisie—can be compared to squatters, organic farmers, punks, the metropolitan hunter-gatherers of the underground resistance. The remaining species of truly wild animals, like dolphins, caribou, and penguins, are analogous to the very, very few existing indigenous peoples of the world who have not yet lost all their culture or been placed in zoos. For all of them, the future looks bleak, as the iron wind of standardization blows across this planet.

All this is not to say that we've deviated from some great plan set out for us by "Mother Nature," or that the measure of happiness and health should be our conformity to the "natural." Whenever human beings try to describe what "Nature" is, they invariably project onto it the laws their own society abides by, or ascribe to it everything they think their civilization lacks; and besides, nature itself is something that changes constantly: at this point, the natural habitat of a poodle really *is* a leash and a kennel. If we have destroyed the natural world with our "civilization," then in the final analysis this must too have been a part of our "natural" destiny (for what is there that does not proceed ultimately from nature? Is humanity somehow blessed or cursed with powers that are . . . *supernatural?*). The question is not how to get back into submission to the Natural, but rather how to reintegrate ourselves into the world around us in a way that *works*. Can we make a world in which humans and animals can live in harmony with each other, with no divisions between them, no distinction between the natural and the civilized, between the familiar and the foreign? Can we escape from the forests of steel into the lush, green ones that linger, atavistic, in our fantasies?

"You [white folks] have not only altered and malformed your winged and four-legged cousins; you have done it to yourselves. You have changed men into chairmen of boards, into office workers, into time-clock punchers. You have changed your women into housewives, truly fearful creatures. I was once invited to the house of one.

"'Watch the ashes, don't smoke, you'll stain the curtains. Watch the goldfish bowl, don't lean your head against the wallpaper; your hair may be greasy. Don't spill liquor on that table: it has a delicate finish. You should have wiped your boots; the floor was just varnished. Don't don't don't...' That is crazy....You live in prisons you have built for yourselves, calling them 'homes, offices, factories.'"

-John (Fire) Lame Deer and Richard Erdoes,
Lame Deer Seeker of Visions

THE QUEEN OF DRAG KINGS ENTERS A SUFI PARADISE

sabelle Eberhardt, disguised as a young Arab man, advances across the southern Algerian desert toward Touggourt, with an entourage of hundreds of men and women dressed in full, elaborate desert costumes. The smell of gunpowder in the air and the raucous noise of pipes and drums accompanies them as they slowly travel on horse back and camel to meet El Hachemi, the Sheikh of a nomadic Sufi sect that Isabelle had secretly joined, and his entourage. As they approach the Sheikh, they find him wearing, in contrast to the colorful crowd, the aus-

The *fantasia* lasted two days and Isabelle remains the only European woman to have ever have experienced such an event. She was 23 years old. Isabelle was born to an exiled Russian aristocrat mother and an Armenian anarchist-disguised-as-priest father in Switzerland in 1877. Her father raised her as an anarchist in a villa compound outside of Geneva; by the time she was sixteen he had taught her to speak Russian, French, German, and Italian, and to read the Koran in Arabic. At nineteen years old she moved to Geneva where she worked as a secretary for

"Life is here."
– Isabelle in her diaries one month before her sudden death.

tere, undecorated green silk robes, green turban and white veil appropriate to a descendent of the prophet El Djilani. The crowd hails him with cries of "Ya O Djilani!" as he attempts to control his white steed. The surrounding sterile dunes seem to come alive with people. Several entourages of horses, aloof camels, and regal desert nomads meet up in a haze of smoke as colorful banners are unfurled with shouts and horses stamps with impatience. Once everyone is assembled they all move to a vast plain covered with tombs, where the riders and horses (Isabelle among them full of fearlessness and anticipation), quickening to the sense of opening space ahead, finally let rip in a headlong gallop, racing, Isabelle wrote later, "as if to the ends of the Earth."

an exiled group of Russian terrorists. At night she began disguising herself as a young sailor boy and was free to explore the darkest corners of Victorian Geneva, crawling from one seedy tavern to the next.

At twenty years old, longing to escape suffocating Europe and to seek the mythical African landscapes she had always dreamed of, she traveled in disguise to northern Algeria, posed as a young male Arab scholar. There, feeling the freedom of her first true independence, Isabelle took lovers of all sorts, in blatant defiance of the stifling European mores of the time. After a brief period of pleasure and perfecting the local Arabic dialect, she joined her fellow students in a brief uprising against the French colonial police in the Mediterranean city of Bône. Armed with a dagger and a pistol she wounded and killed at least one officer in the street battles that consumed the city. To escape possible arrest, Isabelle went into hiding, eventually surfacing in Paris months later as a journalist of "Turkish" descent. Longing for the desert, which she hadn't reached on her first trip, she soon returned in secret, again disguised as an Arab male. Journeying south to the open plains, she joined a nomadic desert tribe, became a mystic, and got married (to a young Arab warrior). She managed to survive an assassination attempted with a holy sword wielded by an enemy of her Sufi sect—a rival group reportedly funded by the French government in Algeria. Her hired killer was put on trial and Isabelle became well known throughout Algeria. She used her new fame to get another journalism assignment, this time for a French-Algerian newspaper. Her fame also brought her greater danger, seeing as she was under investigation by the governments of France, Switzerland, and Russia for various nefarious activities. Therefore, she decided to follow the French army invading the remote frontier of Morocco. But Isabelle soon began neglecting her assignment when she came into contact with a Sufi mystic in a hidden mountain fortress near the border. She disappeared for several months— lost in which worlds, we cannot say.

She surfaced in an oasis town, sick and exhausted: Isabelle's body had been ravaged by her intense life. Shortly thereafter, at the age of 27, Isabelle died in a flash flood.

Isabelle's participation in the desert *fantasia* and her life story as a whole remind us all that escaping our colonialist (and now tourist) mindsets whilst wandering our Earth is absolutely possible, and can lead us into worlds we had only hoped to imagine. If we were to even dare a fraction of the passionate and relentless seekings of Isabelle we would find our little worlds exploding outward before us. Her "drift" (which led her to the desert) also evokes the adage that, indeed, once you leave the safety of your air conditioned tour bus (or your *Let's Go!* Travel Guide for that matter!) there is no going home again . . . as you may have already guessed.

ART GETS FUCKED ON PAGE 108

is for Freedom

I rode a bike yesterday, for the first time in months. It took me over every obstacle we found in our path. We sped over bumps and around sharp curves together, down narrow streets and through wide squares paved with cobblestones. I felt the wind, and was more like a bird than a person, blessed with the gift of flight. I was weightless and powerful; I had left myself suddenly to enter the world, to be open to those tall spires and cramped alleys; yet I was somehow more myself than I had been in a long time, as if I had been passing through a vast desert. I feel strong, my love, and not just because of the bike. I feel sometimes like I'm doing the right thing.

Freedom is a sensation. We have only "choice."

It's almost ludicrous to think of how many men and women have fought and died for the American idea of freedom: a man in a voting booth with a pencil, choosing which box to check. Real freedom, the kind of freedom we are fighting for, is something much grander—it means creating the choices you choose *between*, for starters. A better illustration is the musician in the act of playing with her companions: in joyous, seemingly effortless cooperation, they actively create the sonic and emotional environment in which they exist, participating thus in the transformation of the world which will in turn transform them. Take this model and extend it to every moment of our lives—now *that* would be real freedom.

Nothing is true, everything is permitted.

In summer of 1999, CrimethInc. special agent Tristran Tzarathustra, who had eaten only garbage all year as a consequence of his oath not to participate in, add fuel to, or encourage in any way the economy of world capitalism, was persuaded by one of his lovers to let her treat him to dinner at an expensive Italian restaurant. In the months before this night, he had nearly starved to death; and living in a city with seductively packaged food leering from every shop window, he had been able to remain faithful to his vow only by constantly browbeating himself with the reminder that any compromise was a capitulation to the system that was starving millions of others.

The experience of breaking this ban terrified him because he wasn't ready for the overwhelming feeling of liberation that surged through him at the moment when he raised his fork. It felt as if the world should end, but did not; or rather, the whole world *did* end, soundlessly, and a new one began, unthinkable, unbearable in its perfect resemblance to the old one; but now he was eating expensive polenta beside his bitter enemies, as if it was nothing.

The horrifying *possibilities* of this world opened again before him, like they had in his youth—the fact that anything could happen, that he could do anything, kill people, leap off buildings, defy any self-regulation or expectation—and he realized with dread that his soul was rejoicing within him, heedless of the disapproval of his conscience. He leaped from his seat and dashed into the streets, and remained pacing them for many hours, agonizing over this rift within himself. At exactly two minutes after midnight he had an epiphany, and rushed home to write these notes:

Freedom is to be found only in the sensation of acting, of self - (and thus world-) creation, of the realization through practice the old saying "nothing is true, everything is permitted." [Example: the revolutionary finds freedom in the experience of totally transforming society, and thereby making himself - not simply in the removal of restrictive forces.] To experience this, one must be capable of doing anything at any time — remember the story of Achilles and the tortoise:

The tortoise asks Achilles: "Are you free, Achilles?" and Achilles responds: "Of course I'm free! I'm Achilles, a god among men, and free men at that. I can do anything I want!"

"So," queries the tortoise, "could you kill me?"

"Easily! I am Achilles, the invulnerable" [Not so, as it turned out, but anyway] "hero of Greek myth and legend, and you are … a tortoise."

"So — kill me," challenges the tortoise, matter-of-factly.

"But you are my steadfast friend, my bosom companion, my comrade! I could never kill you!" protests Achilles!

"Exactly," whispers the tortoise suggestively, and Achilles shudders.

The moral is that in a situation where all meaning is already attributed, freedom is irrelevant, for all your possible actions are already determined. Freedom is to be found only in new spaces, in the brand new moments when fresh elements come into play and you have to create yourself from scratch.

One must remain in practice if one is to be a revolutionary: must constantly destroy and recreate the self, must push limits and break every rule and limitation (thus the otherwise inexplicable affection so many freedom-lovers have had for the marquis de Sade)—just as Jane E. wrote in her pamphlet on hypocrisy.

The problem with all this is that the exercise of total freedom is bound to conflict with your own desires. In addition to feeling the sensation of freedom from all constraints and having healthy food in my stomach, I also really do desire never to compromise with those motherfuckers, never to treat animal or dairy products as if they were food, never to give them my money or anyone else's …

The answer to all this, of course, is simply that we must create a world in which everything that is possible is also desirable - so that such a thing as "sin" will no longer even be conceivable, and there will be no reason for guilt, no possibility of hypocrisy or conflict between desires. In the utopia our revolution (mythically speaking, now) should create, anything will be possible — and good, for our hearts demand nothing less than total freedom. I shouldn't have to resist anything, any temptation; therefore I must make a world of temptation without shame — a world empty of meat and dairy products and fancy, elitist bourgeois restaurants, for example!

is for Gender

> *"Men look at women; women watch themselves being looked at."*
> –Simone de Boudoir

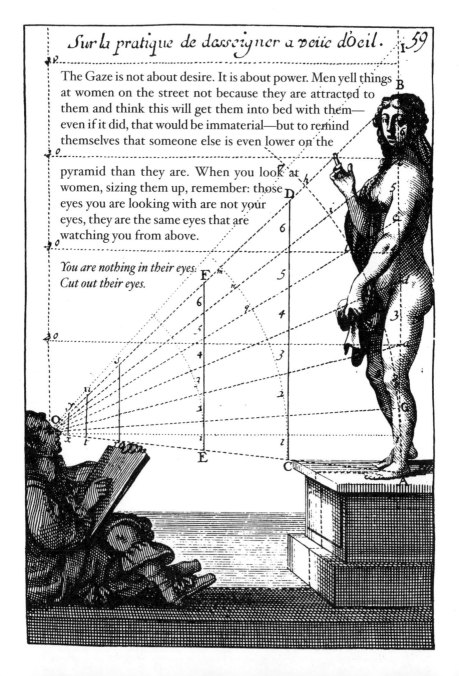

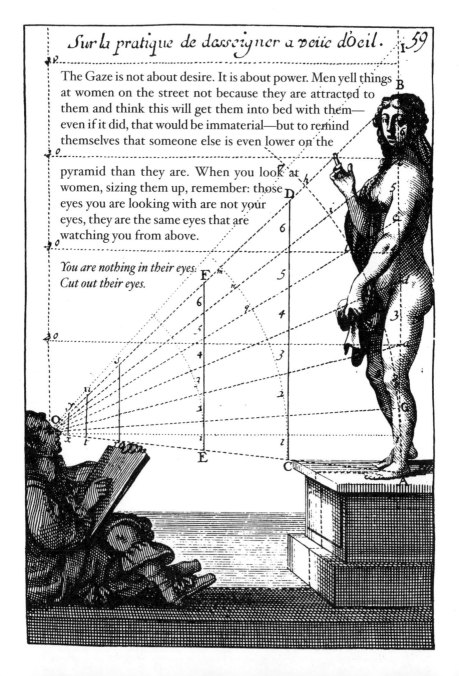

The Gaze is not about desire. It is about power. Men yell things at women on the street not because they are attracted to them and think this will get them into bed with them— even if it did, that would be immaterial—but to remind themselves that someone else is even lower on the pyramid than they are. When you look at women, sizing them up, remember: those eyes you are looking with are not your eyes, they are the same eyes that are watching you from above.

You are nothing in their eyes. Cut out their eyes.

Sur la pratique de dasseigner a veiie d'oeil. 159

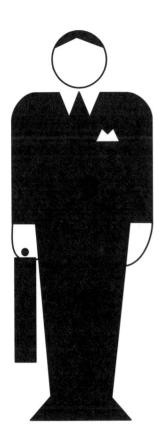

You can see in the very movements of their bodies, forced painfully into the narrow space of permitted masculinity, moving inside an invisible cage, how the supposed winners of the gender game suffer just as much as the others from their hollow victory. Constantly terrified of each other and everyone else, themselves most of all, they take their fear out on the rest of us, perpetuating the climate of fear and violence—but when the terrain of affection itself has been occupied, when every gesture has been appropriated by the language of coercion, how will we approach each other for support, for sanctuary and for healing?

Gender is another false division of life into arbitrary categories, none of which can adequately describe or contain any of us, in order to define us against each other in the interests of Power. There is no male. There is no female. Get free. Go off the map.

ART EXPLODES ITSELF

In a Zurich nightclub, a motley crue of draft dodgers, petty criminals, failed mathematicians, and would-be poets with speech impediments gathered to demystify and ultimately destroy Art as a category separate from life. Their careless assault on Western civilization set the standard for many cultural guerrilla warrior tribes of the 20th century (including New York's Up Against the Wall Motherfuckers, the self-described "streetgang with an analysis").

When speaking to a polite audience of academics decades later, Dada Lama Richard Huelsenbeck was asked if dada developed as a reaction to the first World War. He responded:

"We were for the war, and today we are still for war. Life must hurt, there are not enough tragedies."

. . . too many farces, not enough tragedies . . .

A REAL WEEKEND WARRIOR ON PAGE 119

is for History, Hygiene, and Hypocrisy

The Dead Hand of the Past

HISTORY

Remember how differently time passed when you were twelve years old? One summer was a whole lifetime, and each day passed as a month does for you now. For everything was new: each day held experiences and emotions that you had never encountered before, and by the time that summer was over you had become a different person. Perhaps you felt a wild freedom then that has since deserted you: you felt as if anything could happen, as if your life could end up being virtually anything at all. Now, deeper into that life, it doesn't seem so unpredictable. The things that were once new and transforming have long since lost their freshness and danger, and the future ahead of you seems to have already been determined by your past.

It is thus that each of us is dominated by history: the past lies upon us like a dead hand, guiding and controlling as if from the grave. At the same time as it gives the individual a conception of herself, an "identity," it piles weight upon her that she must fight to shake off if she is to remain light and free enough to continue reinventing herself. It is the same for the artist: even the most challenging innovations eventually become crutches and clichés. Once an artist has come up with one good solution for a creative problem, it is hard for her to break free of it to conceive of other possible solutions. That is why most great artists can only offer a few really revolutionary ideas: they become trapped by the very systems they create, just as these systems trap those who come after. It is hard to do something entirely new when one finds oneself up against a thousand years of painting history and tradition. And this is the same for the lover, for the mathematician and the adventurer: for all, the past is an adversary to action in the present, an ever-increasing force of inertia that must be overcome.

It is the same for the radical, too. Conventional wisdom has it that a knowledge of the past is indispensable in the pursuit of freedom and social change. But today's radical thinkers and activists are no closer to changing the world for their knowledge of past philosophies and struggles; on the contrary, they often seem mired in ancient methods and arguments, unable to apprehend what is needed in the present to make things happen. Their place in the tradition of struggle has trapped them in a losing battle, defending positions long useless and outmoded; their constant references to the past not only render them incomprehensible to others, but also prevent them from referencing what is going on around them.

Let's consider what it is about history that makes it so paralyzing. In the case of world history, it is the exclusive, anti-subjective nature of the thing: History (with a capital "H") is purportedly seen by the

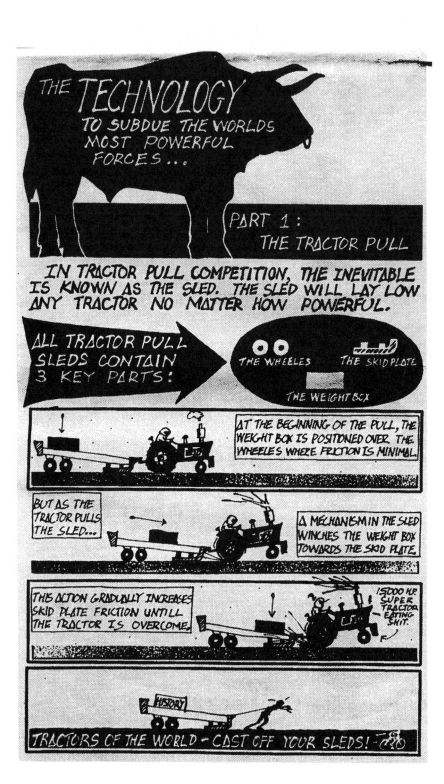

Those who cannot forget the past are condemned to repeat it.

objective eye of science, as if "from above;" it demands that the individual value her impressions and experiences less than the official Truth about the past. But it is not just official history that paralyzes us, it is the very idea of the past itself.

Try thinking of the world as including all past and future time as well as present space. An individual can at least hope to have some control over that part of the world which is in the future; but the past only acts on her, she can never act back upon it. If she thinks of the world (whether that "world" consists of her life, or human history) as consisting of mostly future, proportionately speaking, she will see herself as fairly free to choose her own destiny and exert her will upon the world. But if her world-view places most of the world in the past, that puts her in a position of powerlessness: not only is she unable to act upon or create most of world in which she exists, but what future does remain is already largely predetermined by the effects of events past.

Who, then, would want to be a meaningless fleck near the end of the eight thousand year history of human civilization? Conceiving of the world in such a way can only result in feelings of futility and predetermination. We must think of the world differently to escape this trap—we must instead place our selves and our present day existence where they rightfully belong, in the center of our universe, and shake off the dead weight of the past. Time may well extend before and behind us infinitely, but that is not how *we* experience the world, and that is not how we must visualize it either, if we want to find any meaning in it. If we dare to throw ourselves into the unknown and unpredictable, to continually seek out situations that force us to *be* in the present moment, we can break free of the feelings of inevitability and inertia that constrain our lives—and, in those instants, step *outside* of history.

What does it mean to step outside of history? It means, simply, to step into the present, to step into yourself. Time is compressed to the moment, space is concentrated to one point, and the unprecedented *density* of life is exhilarating. The rupture that occurs when you shake off everything that has come before is not just a break with the past—you are ripping yourself out of the past-future continuum you had built, hurling yourself into a vacuum where *anything* can happen and you are forced to remake yourself according to a new design. It is a sensation as terrifying as it is liberating, and nothing false or superfluous can survive it. Without such purges, life becomes so choked up with the dead and dry that it is nearly unlivable—as it is for us, today.

None of this is to say that we should condone the deliberate lies of those who would *rewrite* history, with the intention of trapping us even deeper in ignorance and passivity than we are now. But the solution is not to combat their supposed "objective truths" with more claims to Historical Truth—for it is not *more* past we need, to weigh upon us, but more attention to today. We must not allow them to make our lives and thoughts revolve only around what has been; instead we must realize that it is up to us to reveal what is true about the present and what is possible from here.

So what can we embrace in place of History? Myth. Not the obscurist superstitions and holy lies of religion and capitalism, but the democratic myths of storytellers. Myth makes no claims to false impartiality or objective Truth, it does not purport to offer an exhaustive explanation of the cosmos. Myth belongs to everyone, as it is made and remade by everyone, so it can never be used by one group to lord itself over another. And it does not paralyze—instead of trapping people in the chains of cause and effect, myth makes them conscious of the enormous range of possibilities that their own lives have to offer; instead of making them feel hopelessly small in a vast and uncaring universe, it centers the world again on their own experiences and ambitions as represented by those of others. When we tell tales around the fire at night of heroes and heroines, of other struggles and adventures and societies, we are offering each other examples of just how much living is possible.

Myth=History Without Time.

The Power of Myth in Action: An Example

To understand how myths work, let's take a look at the sub-counterculture of punk rock. Punk history doesn't need to be "remembered" (i.e., written down for everyone by the experts), for it is all *present* every time a punk band plays and, drawing on a tradition longer than any of us could possibly remember, recaptures that ageless, timeless frenzy that makes punk rock matter in the first place. The facts and details of the past are absolutely irrelevant, and could not themselves enable any band to do this; the band must simply recognize the timeless, crucial element that made their predecessors' music matter, and learn from them that it cannot be caught the same way twice. All those punk history books just weigh you down, and become obviously immaterial when a band is in front of you *doing it.* That passion you can still see in the wild abandon of the best punk bands is an ahistorical force if anything is—it isn't something that can be explained in terms of history and tradition: what they are drawing on is above all *a tradition of violating tradition,* of breaking taboos in order to broaden the world. Thus, when it works, the myth of the punk band that destroys and liberates through music is not a restrictive Platonic archetype, not a confining "identity," but a model that *enables* action.

There may be those who will threaten that the whole world will unravel if we stop concerning ourselves with the past and think only of the present. Let it unravel, then! A lot of good history has done us until now, repeating and repeating itself. Let's break out of it once and for all, before we too tread the circular path that our ancestors have worn so bare.

Let's make the leap out of History, and make the moments of our daily lives the world we live in and care about—only then can we make it into a place that has meaning for us. The present belongs to those who are able to seize it, to recognize all that it is and can be!

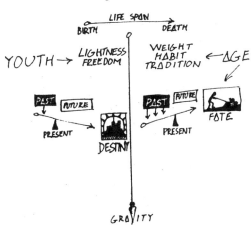

How to Break the Chain of Events (time travel and other banalities)

The world of real life, of the raw urgency of the moment, waits for us beneath history, its mysteries passed down through generations in the currency of experiences so intense they seem to transcend time itself. These experiences can be suppressed, discouraged and denied by the clocks that tick at us from every side, but as long as we

Have you ever noticed—
the more clocks we have,
the less time?

Yes, I've had my moments—but I would have liked for my life to have been nothing but moments, one after another . . .

have hearts in our chests, we will find our ways to them again and again. History is haunted by its own karma; the moment of revolution, of real poetry, brings all its unsettled debts back into play, to be discharged forever so life can really begin. What we need now are instants so overwhelming, so irresistible, that the entire control system of regulated time melts beneath their scorching radiance. We adventurers should track these instants through this world as hunters track the most prized of prey.

We want to *live*, to be *here, now*. A desire that goes beyond the present, past, future, atemporal, an instant that hangs in infinity like a single musical note, like our stories and scars that remain regardless of our second thoughts. *Today I feel and exist, forever.* Against the clocks. Amen.

Postscript: If Not Now, Then When?

Man must live every day, or he will not live at all. His joy and freedom must be a part of everyday life.

Whatever solution, whatever revolution, we propose, must be present-oriented rather than future-oriented if it is to be genuinely revolutionary.

Christianity demands of its followers that they delay gratification until they enter the next world, when they will supposedly be rewarded for their proper conduct; in doing so it assumes that this proper conduct is not fulfilling enough in itself to be worthwhile unless it is rewarded. This kind of thinking reflects a dire misunderstanding of the nature of human happiness; for happiness is to be found in *activity*, in activities that are exciting and satisfying in and of themselves, rather than in awaiting rewards for unsatisfying activities. Therefore it is not surprising that many devout Christians are bitter, spiteful individuals who jealously resent healthy activity and excitement in others—for they believe that they will find true happiness only in their "heavenly reward" for behavior that is not at all exciting for them, and thus must watch enviously as others freely do what they can only dream of doing in their most "sinful" fantasies. Conversely, many Christians who are happy are happy despite their Christianity, because they are able to take pleasure in their lives and deeds in this world.

Traditional Marxism takes the Christian mistake one step further by asking its adherents to work towards a revolution they will probably never live to see—that is, in the Marxist "faith," gratification is delayed beyond the reach of human experience. It should be no surprise that today, beyond a little anachronistic romanticism about the "nobility" of self-sacrifice, the Marxist offer serves as little incentive for people to seriously fight for the "communist revolution." In contrast, today's capitalistic consumer market at least promises prompt gratification in the form of material goods (and the myths and images it associates with them) in return for the generally unsatisfying labor it requires.

Our revolution must be an *immediate* revolution in our daily lives; anything else is *not* a revolution, but a demand that once again people do what they do not want to do and hope that *this* time, somehow, the compensation will be enough. Those who assume, often unconsciously, that it is impossible to achieve their own desires—and thus, that it is futile to fight for themselves—often end up fighting for an ideal or cause instead. But it *is* still possible to fight for ourselves (or at least the experiment must be worth a try); so it is crucial that we seek change not in the name of some doctrine or grand cause, but on behalf of ourselves, so that we will be able to live more meaningful lives. Similarly, we must seek first and foremost to alter the contents of our own lives in a revolutionary manner, rather than direct our struggle towards world-historical changes which we will not live to witness. In this way we will avoid the feelings of worthlessness and alienation that result from believing that it is necessary to "sacrifice oneself for the cause," and instead live to experience the fruits of our labors . . . *in our labors themselves*.

SHORT-LIVED ANARCHIST STATE IN FIUME

Gabriel D'Annunzio, Decadent poet, artist, musician, aesthete, womanizer, pioneer daredevil aeronautist, black magician, genius and cad, emerged from World War I as a hero with a small army at his beck and command: the "Arditi." At a loss for adventure, he decided to capture the city of Fiume from Yugoslavia and give it to Italy. After a necromantic ceremony with his mistress in a cemetery in Venice, he set out to conquer Fiume, and succeeded without any trouble to speak of. But Italy turned down his generous offer; the Prime Minister called him a fool.

In a huff, D'Annunzio decided to declare independence and see how long he could get away with it. He and one of his anarchist friends wrote the constitution, which declared music to be the central principle of the State. The Navy (made up of deserters and Milanese maritime unionists) named themselves the Uscochi, after the long-vanished pirates who once lived on lo-cal offshore islands and preyed on Venetian and Ottoman shipping. These modern Uscochi succeeded in some wild coups—several rich Italian merchant vessels suddenly gave the Republic a future: money in the coffers! Artists, bohemians, adventurers, anarchists (D'Annunzio corresponded with Malatesta), fugitives and Stateless refugees, homosexuals, military dandies (the uniform was black with pirate skull and crossbones—later stolen by the S.S.) and crank reformers of every stripe (including Buddhists, Theosophists, and Vedantists) began to show up at Fiume in droves. The party never stopped. Every morning D'Annunzio read poetry and manifestos from his balcony; every evening a concert, then fireworks. This made up the entire activity of the government. Eighteen months later, when the wine and money had run out and the Italian fleet finally showed up and lobbed a few shells at the Municipal Palace, no one had the energy to resist.🐾

A PAUPER'S SYMPHONY DEBUTS ON PAGE 126

hygiene

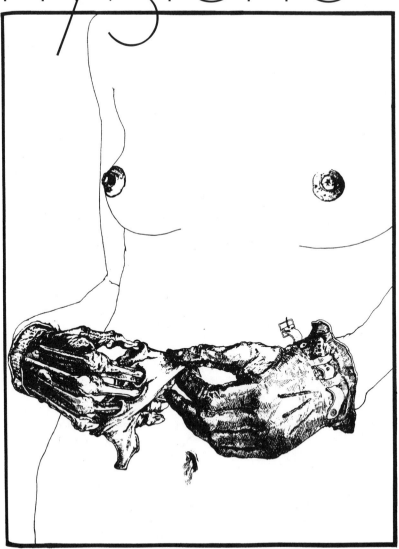

"The remaining noticeable characteristic of "Che" is his filth. He hates to wash and will never do so. He is filthy, even by the rather low standard of cleanliness prevailing among the Castro forces in the Sierra Maestra. Once in a while, "Che" would take some of his men to a stream or pool, in order that they might wash. On those occasions "Che" would never wash either himself or his clothes, but would sit on the bank and watch the others. He is really outstandingly and spectacularly dirty."
-slanderous description of Ernesto "Che" Guevara
from the 1958 C.I.A. dossier

washing . . . and brainwashing

Even in the most anti-establishment of underground circles, I'm amazed by how frequently I hear people complain about people they call "hippies" or "crusty punks." "These crusty punks came in here and smelled up the whole place," they'll say. What great transgression have these people committed to be so reviled? They have a different orientation to the question of "cleanliness" than the rest of us do.

Where do our ideas and values about so-called "cleanliness" come from, anyway? Western civilization has a long history of associating cleanliness with goodness and merit, best summed up by the old expression "cleanliness is next to Godliness." In ancient Greek plays, evil people and spirits—the Furies, for example—were often described as filthy. The Furies were dirty, aged, and female, exactly the opposite of how the playwright who described them saw himself; their filthiness, among other things, identified them as an outgroup—as alien, animal, inhuman. Over time, cleanliness became a measure with which the haves separated themselves from the have-nots. Those who possessed the wealth and power required to have the leisure to remain indoors, inactive, scorned the peasants and travelers whose lifestyles involved getting their hands and bodies dirty. Throughout our history, we can see that cleanliness has been used as a standard of worth by those with power to ascribe social status—and thus, the "Godly," the self-proclaimed holy ones who stood above the rest of us in hierarchical society, proclaimed that their cleanliness, bought with the labor of the others who were forced to work for them, was a measure of their "Godliness" and superiority. To this day, we accept this traditional belief: that being "clean" according to social norms is desirable in itself.

It should be clear from the history of our ideas about "cleanliness" that anyone who is critical of mainstream values, any radical or punk rocker, should be extremely suspicious of the great value placed on being "clean" according to traditional standards. Besides, what exactly does "clean" mean?

These days, cleanliness is defined more by corporations selling "sanitation products" than by anyone else. This is important to keep in mind. Certainly, most of these products have an uncanny ability to cut through natural dirt and grime—but does removing natural dirt and grime with synthetic chemicals necessarily constitute the only acceptable form of sanitation? I'm at least as frightened by these manufactured, artificial products as I am of a little dust, mud, or sweat, or (god forbid!) a stain from food or blood on my shirt. At least I know where the "filth" came from, and what it's made of!

The idea that it is worthwhile to use chemicals (whether they be deodorant, detergent, or shampoo) to eradicate organic dirt has some frightening implications, too. First, it supports the old Christian superstition that the biological body is shameful and should be hidden—that our bodies and our existence in the physical world as animals are intrinsically disgusting and sinful. This valuation has been used to keep us insecure and ashamed, and thus at the mercy of the priests and other authorities who tell us how to become "pure": once, by submitting to their holy denial of the self, and now, by spending plenty of our money on the various "sanitation" products they want to sell us. Also, as capitalism transforms the entire world from the organic (forests, swamps, deserts, rivers) to the inorganic (cities of concrete and steel, suburbs of asphalt and astroturf, wastelands that have been stripped of all natural resources, garbage dumps) the idea that there is something more worthwhile about synthetic chemicals than natural dirt implies that this transformation might actually be a good thing... and thus implicitly justifies their profit-motivated destruction of our planet.

In reality, these corporations are far less concerned with our health and cleanliness than they are with selling us their products. They use the high value we place on sanitation to sell us all sorts of products in its name... and who knows what the real, long-term health effects of these products are? *They* certainly don't care. If we do eventually get sick from using their special cleansers and hi-tech shampoos, they

can just sell us another product—medicine—and keep the wheels of the capitalist economy turning. And the shame about our bodies (as producers of sweat and other natural fluids which we deem "dirty") that they capitalize on and encourage also aids them in selling us other products which depend upon our insecurity: diet products, exercise products, fashionable clothes, etc. When we accept their definition of "cleanliness" we are accepting their economic domination of our lives.

Even if they agree about the questionable nature of today's sanitation products, most people today would still argue that sanitation is still healthier than filth. To some extent this is true—it probably is a good idea to wash your feet if you step in shit. But aside from obvious cases like that, there are a thousand different standards of what is clean and what is dirty across the world; if you look at different societies and civilizations, you come across health practices that seem suicidal by our sanitation standards. And yet, these people survive as well as we do. People in Africa a few hundred years ago lived comfortably in a natural environment that destroyed many of the very prim and polished Western explorers that came to their continent. Human beings can adapt to a wide variety of environments and situations, and it seems that the question of what kinds of sanitation are healthy

Eight Reasons Why Capitalists Want to Sell You Deodorant.

1. Body smells are erotic and sexual. Capitalists don't like that because they are impotent and opposed to all manifestations of sensuality and sexuality. Sexually awakened people are potentially dangerous to capitalists and their rigid, asexual system.

2. Body smells remind us that we are animals. Capitalists don't want us to be reminded of that. Animals are dirty. They eat things off the ground, not out of plastic wrappers. They are openly sexual. They don't wear suits or ties, and they don't get their hair done. They don't show up to work on time.

3. Body smells are unique. Everyone has her own body smell. Capitalists don't like individuality. There are millions of body smells but only a few deodorant smells. Capitalists like that.

4. Some deodorants are harmful. Capitalists like that because they are always looking for new illnesses to cure. Capitalists love to invent new medicines. Medicines make money for them and win them prizes; they also cause new illnesses so capitalists can invent even more new medicines.

5. Deodorants cost you money. Capitalists are especially pleased about that.

6. Deodorants hide the damage that capitalist products cause your body. Eating meat and other chemical-filled foods sold by capitalists makes you smell bad. Wearing pantyhose makes you smell bad. Capitalists don't want you to stop wearing pantyhose or eating meat.

7. Deodorant-users are insecure. Capitalists like insecure people. Insecure people don't start trouble. Insecure people also buy room fresheners, hair conditioners, makeup, and magazines with articles about dieting.

8. Deodorants are unnecessary. Capitalists are very proud of that and they win marketing awards for it.

is at least as much a question of convention as of hard-set biological rules. Try violating a few of the "common sense" rules of Western sanitation some time: you'll find that eating out of garbage cans and going a few weeks without a shower aren't really as dangerous or difficult as we were taught.

Perhaps the most important question when it comes to the unusual value we place on traditional "cleanliness" is what we lose by doing this. Once, before we covered up our natural scents with chemicals, each of us had a unique smell. These scents attracted us to each other and bound us emotionally to each other through memory and association. Now, if you have positive associations with the scent of the man you love, it is probably his cologne (identical to the cologne of thousands of other men) that you enjoy, not his own personal scent. And the natural pheromones with which we once communicated with each other, which played such an important role in our sexuality, are now completely smothered by standardized chemical products. We no longer know what it is like to be pure, natural human beings, to smell like real human beings. Who knows how much we may have lost because of this? Those who find me disgusting for enjoying the scent and taste of my lover when she hasn't showered or rubbed synthetics all over herself, when she smells like a real human being, are probably the same ones who shudder at the idea of digging a vegetable out of the ground and eating it instead of the plastic-wrapped, man-made fast food that we have all been brought up on. We have become so accustomed to our domesticated, engineered existence that we don't even know what we're missing.

So try to be a little more open minded when it comes to the "crusties." Perhaps they just smell bad to you because you've never gotten a chance to discover what a real human being smells like; perhaps there is something worthwhile about being "unwashed" that you haven't noticed before. The moral of this story is the moral of all anarchist stories: accept only the rules and values which really make sense to you. Figure out what's right for you and don't let anybody tell you different—but also, make an effort to understand where others are coming from, and evaluate their actions by your own standards, not according to some standardized norm.

THE CONCERT AT BAKU

On this day Russian experimental composer Arseny Mikhailovich Avraamov ascended to the roof of a tall building and directed a concert of factory sirens, steam whistles, artillery, and everything else in the city of Baku capable of making loud noise; for the climax of the piece, the entire fleet of the Caspian Sea joined in with their foghorns.

Although the Bolshevik government soon tightened the controls on artists of every field, for a short time the upheaval of the Russian revolution made new applications of the arts like this possible[3]. Prior to the revolution, Avraamov had lived in abject poverty and obscurity, unable even to afford a piano on which to test out his compositions; he would walk around Baku, looking in garbage cans for food, gazing with envy and desperation at the rich men around him and the pet "artists" who followed them like trained poodles. It was an impossible dream to him to think that one day he might not only be fed and housed in return for offering his creativity to society (rather than his alienated labor), but also be given the opportunity to utilize all of its resources in doing this. But the revolutionary government that took power in Baku took the communists at their word that everyone should be equally empowered to contribute to society in her own way, that the means of production should belong to the people as a whole and be used to make life more pleasurable for everyone; knowing that Avraamov was a struggling artist with avant garde pretensions, they commissioned him to write a symphony celebrating the liberation of the city, that could be played upon the machinery of the city itself.

Riding around on the new public transport, conferring with factory foremen about whistle pitch and timing, the young artist had a brief taste of what could happen if the arts were taken seriously as a means of improving life, not just imitating it. Later, Avraamov was to suffer the same restrictions on his work that the centralized Soviet establishment imposed on everyone; but on this day, everyone in Baku was treated to participation in a moving demonstration of what is possible when art and cooperation are considered integral to social life, rather than quarantined to our "private lives" and "leisure" time.☾

---

[3] Another celebrated example of this brief period of freedom and innovation was the invention in 1919 of the Theremin, the first electronic musical instrument, by Lenin's friend Leon Theremin.

---

the 1930's
ANARCHIST REVOLUTION IN SPAIN

You can read about this elsewhere easily enough. It's a good example to bring out, though, when people tell you that a radically democratic/egalitarian society is an impossible dream, and that even if one did exist it could never be defended from outside aggressors.

☞BLOOD SHED IN NOTRE-DAME ON PAGE 132

"The will to a system is the will to a lie." –Jean Genet

Hypocrisy
. . . is the sincerest form of . . .

Today it is impossible to avoid hypocrisy in any struggle against the status quo.

The political and economic structures are constructed so that it is practically impossible to avoid being implicated in their workings. Today, whatever a man thinks of the employment opportunities available to him or of our economic system itself, he has almost no choice except to work if he does not want to starve to death or die of an illness for which he could not afford health care. If he does not believe in material property, he still has no choice but to buy all the food and clothing he needs, and to buy or rent living space (that is, if he is not ready to live at odds with the legal system)—for there is no free land left that has not been claimed by someone, almost no food or other resources anywhere that are not someone's "property." If a woman wants to distribute material criticizing the capitalist system of production and consumption, she still has no way to produce and distribute this material without paying to produce it, and selling it to consumers—or at least selling advertising, which encourages people to be consumers—to finance production. If a woman does not want to finance the brutal torture and slaughter of animals in the name of capitalism, she can stop eating meat and dairy products, stop purchasing health products which are tested on animals, and stop wearing leather and fur; but there are still animal products in the films in her camera and the movies she watches, in the vinyl records she listens to, in countless other products which she will be hard-pressed to do without in modern society. Besides, the companies she buys her vegetables from are most likely connected to the companies who make meat and dairy products, so her money goes to the same ends; and these vegetables themselves were probably picked by migrant work-

I can resist anything, except temptation.

—William Burroughs

ers or other oppressed labor. For the average man, who is unready to uproot his life completely and risk death and complete ostracism, keeping his hands clean of the nightmare around him is an impossible dream.

Even if you radically reject and disconnect yourself from every one of these institutions, and survive by means of theft and transgression alone, you are still playing a role in the status quo. "The System" is a vast, organic entity that includes everything within its boundaries, even the recluses who flee from it and the terrorists who die fighting it. To fight it is *always* to fight it from within, for it creates us and molds us, even when it directs us against itself. To claim to be outside it for even an instant, living as we do in a world that is made up almost entirely of human constructs (whether physical, social, or philosophical) is worse than madness—it is misplaced fanaticism of a decidedly Christian bent.

Modern Western values are so deeply ingrained in our minds that it is practically impossible to avoid being influenced in our actions by the very assumptions and attitudes we are struggling against. After a lifetime of being taught to place a financial value on the hours of our lives, it is hard to stop feeling like one must be rewarded materially for an activity for it to be worthwhile. After a lifetime of being taught to respect hierarchies of authority, it is very difficult to suddenly interact with all human beings as equals—let alone have sex with them without eroticizing domination and submission! After a lifetime of being taught to associate happiness with passive spectatorship, it is hard to enjoy building furniture more than watching television. And of course there are ten thousand more subtle ways in which these values and assumptions manifest themselves in our thoughts and our actions.

This does not mean that resistance is futile—indeed, if our choices today are so limited that we cannot act without replicating the conditions from which we were trying to escape, resistance is all the more crucial. This *does* mean that "innocence" is a myth, a counter-revolutionary concept which we must leave behind us with the rest of post-Christian thinking. The traditional Christian demand upon human beings is that they be *innocent*, that they keep their hands clean of any "sin." At the same time, "sin" is so difficult for the Christian to avoid (as counter-revolutionary activity is today, for us) that this demand leads to feelings of guilt, failure, and ultimately despair when he realizes that it is impossible for him to be "innocent" and "pure." In fact, by forbidding "sin," Christian doctrine makes it all the more tempting and intriguing for the believer; for whether the mind does or not, the human heart recognizes no authority and will always seek out that which is forbidden.

We must not make the same mistakes as the Christians. The demand that radicals be free from hypocrisy, free from any implication in the system, has the same effects as the Christian demand that people be free from sin: it creates frustration and despair in those who would seek change, and at the same time makes hypocrisy all the more tempting. Rather than seek to have clean hands, we should aim to make the inevitable negative effects of our lives *worthwhile* by offering enough positive activity to more than balance the scales. This approach to the problem can save us from being immobilized by fear of hypocrisy or shame about our "guilt."

Besides, demands that we avoid hypocrisy deny the complexity of the human soul. The human heart is not simple; every human being has a variety of desires which pull her in different directions. To ask that she only pursue some of those desires and always ignore others is to demand that she remain perpetually unfulfilled . . . and curious. This is typical of the kind of dogmatic, ideological thinking which has afflicted us for centuries: it insists that the individual *must* be loyal to one set of rules and only one, rather than doing what is appropriate for her needs in a particular situation.

It might well be true that the whole self can only be expressed in hypocrisy. Certainly a person needs to formulate a general set of guidelines regarding the decisions she will make, but to break from these occasionally prevents stagnation and offers the opportunity to consider whether the guidelines need reevaluation. A person who is not afraid to be hypocritical from time to time is in less danger of selling out permanently one day, because she is able to taste the "forbidden fruit" without feeling forced to make a permanent choice. She is immune to the shame and eventual despair that afflict those who strive for perfect "innocence."

So be proud of yourself as you are: don't try to get the inconsistencies of your soul to match up in a false and forced manner, or it will only come back to haunt you. Rather than holding inflexibly to a set system, let us dare to reject the idea that we must be faithful to any particular doctrine in our efforts to create a better life for ourselves. Let us *not* claim to be innocent, let us *not* claim to be pure or right! But let us proclaim proudly that we are hypocrites, that we will stop at nothing, not even hypocrisy, in our struggle to take control of our lives. In this age when it is impossible to avoid being a part of the system we strive against, only blatant hypocrisy is truly subversive—for it alone speaks the truth about our hearts, and it alone can show just how difficult it is to avoid living the modern life which has been prepared for us. And that alone is good reason to fight.

"Nothing smaller than hypocrisy is big enough for me."
—Diane di Prima

Text by Jane E. Humble. Dedicated to every radical who loves wearing leather jackets, riding motorcycles, and being addressed as "slut" or "whore" during sex.

Exhibit A: CrimethInc. Itself "insINC.ere"

The CrimethInc. collective is a perfect example of the difficulties a subversive organization will encounter in seeking to avoid hypocrisy, and of the liberating possibilities that embracing hypocrisy can create.

Our tabloid Harbinger exists to criticize such modern phenomena as advertising, which is fundamentally an effort on the part of modern businesses to persuade people to purchase their products whether or not this is in their best interest. And yet CrimethInc. *must* sell advertising in the pages of Harbinger in order to finance its publication, at least when the proceeds from stolen cars are not enough. Harbinger exists to warn against those who would sell ideologies that prescribe certain kinds of thinking and acting, whether or not these manners of thinking and acting are in the best interest of human beings. And yet, in order to compete with these forces, CrimethInc. too must sell an ideology of sorts: an ideology of "thinking for yourself," but an ideology all the same. Certainly we may claim that *our* products, *our* ideologies, really *are* in the best interest of human beings, but isn't that what every corporation and political party claims?

In this case and a thousand others it is impossible for us in CrimethInc. to pursue the goals we seek without simultaneously betraying those goals. Just as we strive to fight against the system, we replicate it. Selling "revolutionary" ideas is still *selling ideas*, and as long as *buying* and *selling* are taking place, nothing truly revolutionary is happening. Indeed the fact that "revolutionary" ideas are being used to perpetuate the status quo means that whatever resistance there might be is neutralized and assimilated from the start.

On the other hand, activity is better than inactivity, and perhaps the efforts that we make here will still be able to have positive effects; and hopefully our willingness to point out where we are compromised will prevent those compromises from rendering our efforts useless. It *might* be possible to incite genuine to change in the lives of human beings, despite the implication inherent in any kind of activity today; it's worth a try.

Of course, perhaps this sort of idealism will only serve to trick us, with the best of all possible intentions, into betraying the very ideals which we seek to promote. Perhaps we are sealing our own fate by transforming whatever genuine desires for change people may have into ultimately ineffectual activities such as purchasing "revolutionary products" and discussing the ideas of others. Perhaps the advertising we sell in Harbinger will only lead people to purchase the products advertised (and thus be forced to remain trapped in the wage slavery system), rather than harmlessly raising the funds necessary to publish our demand for the end of this system. Or maybe this hypocrisy is merely a cover that allows us to go about our business of revolution without appearing to be much of a threat, by making us appear to be another innocuous, pseudo-revolutionary group; perhaps we only appear to be hopelessly compromised so the forces that have a stake in the status quo will not recognize the threat that we do pose—until it is too late! Or it might even be that CrimethInc. is actually orchestrated by those very forces, to lead those who do desire change astray into expending their efforts uselessly—even then, it might have unforeseen effects. . . Who can tell for sure?

The thing is to *act*, to act joyously, not to accept that we are helpless to effect change. For if we seek to resist the roles and lives set forward for us, if we fight a spirited fight against the forces that would keep us in despair, if we dare to act on our own and to act passionately and freely, that itself is revolution.

THE NOTRE-DAME INCIDENT

Four young men sneaked through the back door into Notre-Dame cathedral, in Paris, during Easter mass. There they quickly divested a Dominican monk of his garments, and one of them—Michel Mourre, who until that point had been a novitiate, studying to be a Dominican himself—dressed in these, then stepped out into the pulpit before an internationally convened crowd of ten thousand people. He addressed them with this sermon:

Today Easter day of the Holy Year
here
under the emblem of Notre-Dame of Paris
I accuse
the universal Catholic Church of the lethal diversion of our living strength toward an empty heaven
I accuse
the Catholic Church of swindling
I accuse
the Catholic Church of infecting the world with its funereal morality
of being the running sore on the decomposed body of the West

Verily I say unto you: God is dead
We vomit the agonizing insipidity of your prayers
for your prayers have been the greasy smoke over the battlefields of our Europe

Go forth then into the tragic and exalting desert of a world where God is dead
and till this earth anew with your bare hands
with your PROUD hands
with your unpraying hands

Today Easter day of the Holy Year
Here under the emblem of Notre-Dame of Paris
we proclaim the death of the Christ-god, so that Man may live at last.

The audience listened in dutiful stupor at first, but then realized what they were hearing and broke into a commotion. The cathedral's Swiss guards drew their swords and rushed to kill the interlopers—one had his face sliced open. His stolen habit soaked with his comrade's blood, Michel cheerfully blessed the screaming crowd as he and his friends escaped out of the cathedral and into crimethinker folklore forever. ❀

ROCK 'N' ROLL RIOT ON PAGE 148!

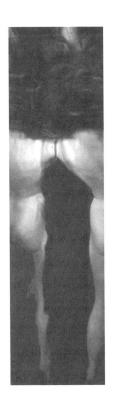

is for Identity, Ideology, and Image

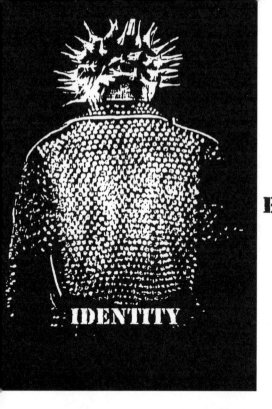

IDENTITY

"US" VERSUS "THEM": THE ETERNAL MYTH AND PARADOX

(adapted from Stella Nera's journals)

1. Identity and the Scarcity Economics of Self

After we met Alec, Jackson remarked: "When I meet a person, I don't like it if he immediately starts talking shit about other people. I don't want to hear about which groups he is against, but what *he* is doing, himself."

Well, Jackson, I think in his own crippled way Alec *was* trying to tell you what he's doing: what he's doing *is* simply "being against" the cliques he was talking about. Perhaps he has no notion of how to do anything more positive than to take an opposing stance. He's certainly not the only one.

Competitive human relations depend on and perpetuate a feeling of impoverishment in the individual, a scarcity economics of the soul: for in the status quo she is unable to do what she wants, and at the same time she *must* feel this helplessness and poverty of life to be willing to play instead the loser's game of power. To assuage this feeling of impoverishment, the individual seeks—more than mere physical possessions, which are just a means to this end—*identity,* the consolation for lack of freedom (if "I can't," at least "I am . . ."). Identity, as a concept, works in terms of contrast: one "is" a fill-in-the-blank, as opposed to the "others," who are not . . . thus, to the desperate lost soul of modern society, nothing is more precious than opponents, people to despise, so he can reassure himself of his own worth: as a faithful patron of brand X ideology, for example. The young "activist," though heretofore unaware of it, has quite a stake in maintaining the *alienation* of others, and it should not be surprising when he acts superior, threatening, etc. in order to maintain the distance between himself and the "normal" people.

To be effective at acting radically (rather than just acting radical!), one must be disinterested in *being* radical or "an activist," but only desire to help make radical things happen. So no more stupid conflicts and infighting, for heaven's sake! In a system which *is* conflict systematized as social relations, in which society is a network of struggles arranged as social structure, *getting along* is practically the definition of the radical act. Until we are able to leave our "identities" behind, whenever we come together it will merely be a case of images meeting and clashing—with the humans behind them unable to even see each other.

2. Fight war and wars

This being the case, we can't spend all our energy on our efforts simply to defeat the State, corporate tyranny, etc.—for even if we do succeed, as long as most people are unable to work together (and thus unaware of their own potential), we can only be another vanguard/ruling party. Under such conditions, the struggle with the state is just another power-struggle substitute for free action. We need to strive simultaneously for freedom from external constraints and for the strength to love and forgive and cooperate, and for this project we absolutely must be ready to shake off our need for Identity in the traditional sense. What we need most now are ways to speak that can *give* others voices of their own (contrary to the aforementioned social scarcity economics, in which the very act of speaking monopolizes expression and denies it to others), ways to act that can activate—these will be the weapons no power can defeat.

What is needed above all, then, is the self-confidence to talk with and listen to others, to find magic tricks by which old conflicts can be superseded and people like Alec and his rival factions discover ways to coexist and support each other. For revolution is not making everyone the same in their ideologies or relations with each other, but simply establishing mutually beneficial relations between different individuals and groups. I would do better myself to think about how Alec and I can transcend our predictable interactions, instead of just analyzing him in a way that makes me feel so much smarter and more mature.

Do you have ideas, or do ideas have you?

"The ideologist is a man who falls for the fraud perpetrated on him by his own intellect: that an idea, i.e. the symbol of a momentarily perceived reality, can possess absolute reality."
—Socrates, refuting Plato's interpretation of his ideas

"I am not a Marxist." —Karl "Groucho" Marx

"The world eludes us because it becomes itself again." —Lewis Carroll

Editor's introduction: Possibly the best text any of us have written on this subject is a letter Nadia once sent to a friend in response to an article he had written with her help (her original title for the piece had been "The Political Struggle is the Struggle Against the Political," which he changed to "Against the Shallowness of the Political")... so here is her letter, reprinted from his private collection. Remember, whatever you believe imprisons you.

• • •

June 2
Amsterdam (at Chloë's, with
Phoebe and Heloise)

Dearest E—,

No, you haven't understood what I'm talking about at *all*. In your hurry to purchase for yourself the image of "political activist" (or, worse, theorist)—whatever that is—you've concluded that *everything* must be "political"—whatever *that* is! For the farther you expand the meaning of any word, the blurrier it becomes, and the more useless. Once *everything* is political, then "political" means nothing all over again, and we have to start from scratch.

So, assuming "political" isn't just a meaningless all-purpose word ... Of course there are "political" ways to look at every issue, including one's own mortality—I wasn't trying to deny *that*. That, in fact, is exactly my point: once you begin to think of yourself as "political," once you start to think in terms of analysis and critique—worse yet to think of yourself as *having* a critique—you come to approach *everything* on those terms, you try to fit *everything* into your analysis. Being

"political" becomes a cancer that slowly spreads to every corner of your being, until you can't think about anything except in terms of class struggle or gender or whatever.

And there is no analysis, no ideology (because that's what we're talking about here, with your insistence on the politics of living and the theory of politics) broad enough to capture everything that life is. An ideology, just like an image, is always something you have to purchase—that is, you must give up a part of yourself in return for it. That part of yourself is every aspect of the world, every deliciously complex experience, every irreducible detail that won't fit into the framework you've so proudly constructed.

Sure, you can look at oral sex and sunsets and love songs and really good Chinese food in terms of political issues, or even approach them in a way that is political in a far less superficial sense—but the fact is that when you're there in those moments there are things that escape any kind of comprehension, let alone expression, let alone analysis. Living and feeling are simply too complicated to be captured completely by any language, or any combination of languages. Just like that fucking halfwit Plato, the casualty of ideology (which I'm begging you not to be) comes to doubt the reality of anything he can't symbolize with language (political or otherwise), because he's forgotten that his symbols are only convenient generalizations to stand in place of the innumerable unique moments that make up the universe.

I can anticipate your response: my critique of the political is itself a political evaluation, a part of my ideology. And so it is. I write to you so vehemently about this because it's an issue I'm really struggling with now. I find myself turning *everything* into a political tract or critique, possessed by (what my ideology describes as!) a capitalistic compulsion to transform all my feelings and experi-

Ambush.

ences into *objects*—that is, into theories I can carry around with me.
My values have come to revolve around these theories, which I show
off as proof of my intelligence and importance, the same way a bourgeois man shows off his car as proof of his worth: my life isn't about
my actual experience anymore, it's about "the struggle"—when I'd
wanted that struggle to be about centering my life on my experiences,
not some new substitute! I'd like to say this letter is my last stand
against the all-consuming demands of the political . . . but that was
probably long ago, the last time I was able to reflect on something
without the political ramifications even occurring to me. Careful what
you wish for, E—, when you say everything is political.

I think part of this pathological need to systematize everything
comes from living in cities, incidentally. Every single thing around us
here has been made by human beings, and has specific human meanings attached to it—so when you look around, instead of seeing the
actual objects that are around you, you see a forest of symbols. When
I was staying in the mountains, it was different. I would go walking
and I wouldn't see "don't walk" signs, I would see trees and flowers,
things that have an existence beyond any framework of human mean-

ings and values. Standing under a starry sky, there, gazing at the silent horizon, the world felt so immense and profound that I could only stand before it mute and trembling. No politics could ever provide a vessel deep enough to hold those moments. Not to say there's no reason for us to conceptualize things, E——, because of course that's useful sometimes . . . but it's a means, and not the only means, to a much greater end. That's all.

I'll leave you with this, my own poor translation of a line from the farewell letter Mao Tse-Tung's mistress wrote him shortly after the so-called success of the Chinese so-called Communist Revolution:

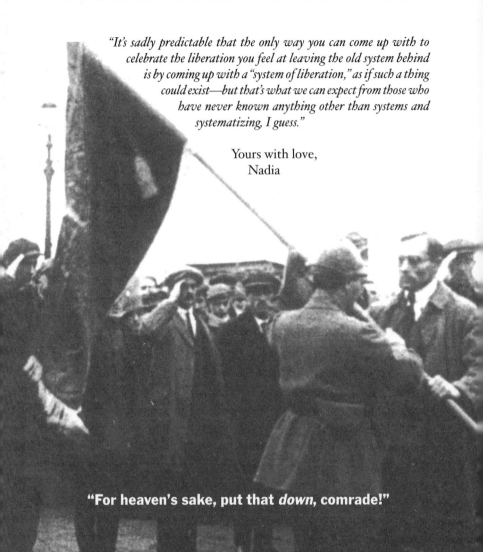

> *"It's sadly predictable that the only way you can come up with to celebrate the liberation you feel at leaving the old system behind is by coming up with a "system of liberation," as if such a thing could exist—but that's what we can expect from those who have never known anything other than systems and systematizing, I guess."*

Yours with love,
Nadia

"For heaven's sake, put that *down*, comrade!"

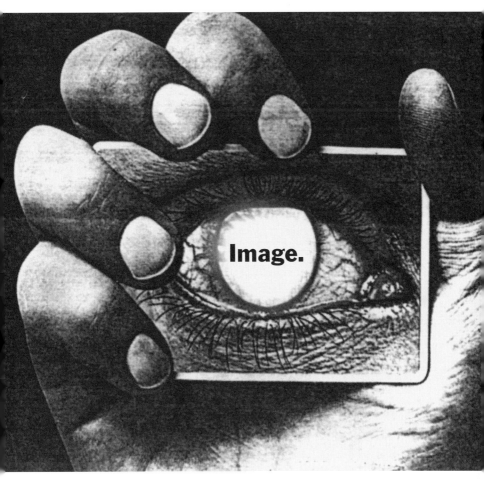

they hold you in the palm of their hand.

Seduced by the Image of Reality

When I would look through magazines as a small child, I used to think that there must be a magical world somewhere where everything looked—and was—perfect. I could see pictures from it in those pages, the smoky air of dimly-lit rooms heavy with drama as the young models lounged in designer fashions. *That* is where excitement and adventure is to be found, I thought, in the world where every room is flawlessly decorated and every woman's wardrobe is picked and

matched with daring and finesse. I resolved to have an adventurous life of my own, and began looking for those rooms and women right away. And though I've discovered since then that romance and excitement rarely come hand in hand with the images of them that are presented to us—usually the opposite is true, that adventure is to be found precisely where there is no time or energy for keeping up appearances—I still catch myself sometimes thinking that everything would be perfect if only I lived in that picturesque log cabin with matching rugs.

Whatever each us may be looking for, we all tend to pursue our desires by pursuing images: symbols of the things we desire. We buy leather jackets when we want rebellion and danger. We purchase fast cars not for the sake of driving at high velocities, but to recapture our lost youth. When we want to live in a different world, we buy political pamphlets and bumper stickers. Somehow we assume that having all the right accessories will get us the perfect lives. And as we construct our lives, we tend to do it according to an image, a pattern that has been laid out for us: hippie, businessman, housewife, punk.

Why do we think so much about images today, rather than concentrating on reality, on our lives and emotions themselves? One of the reasons images have attained so much significance in this society is that, unlike activities, images are easy to sell. Advertising and marketing, which are designed to invest products with a symbolic value that will attract consumers, have transformed our culture. Corporations have been spreading propaganda designed to make us believe in the magic powers of their commodities for generations now: deodorant offers popularity, soda offers youth and energy, jeans offer sex appeal. At our jobs, we exchange our time, energy, and creativity for the ability to buy these symbols—and we keep buying them, for of course no quantity of cigarettes can really give anyone sophistication. Rather than satisfying our needs, these products multiply them: for to get them, we must sell our lives away. We keep going back, not knowing any other way, hoping that the new product (self-help books, punk rock records, that vacation cabin with matching rugs) will be the one that will fix everything.

We are easily persuaded to chase these images because it is simply easier to change the scenery around you than it is to change your own life. How much less trouble, how much less risky it would be if you could make your life perfect just by collecting all the right accessories! No participation necessary. The image comes to embody all the things you desire, and you spend all your time and energy trying to get the details right (the bohemian tries to find the perfect black beret and the right poetry readings to attend—the frat boy has to be seen with the right friends, at the right parties, drinking the right beers and wearing the right informal dress shirts) rather than pursuing the desires themselves—for it is easier to identify yourself with a prefabricated image than to identify exactly what you want in life. But if you really want adventure, an Australian hunting jacket won't suffice—and if you want real romance, dinner and a movie with the most popular girl at your school might not be enough.

Fascinated as we are by images, our values have come to revolve around a world we can never actually experience. There's no way into the pages of the magazine, there's no way to be the archetypal punk or the perfect executive. We're "trapped" out here in the real world, forever. And yet we keep looking for life in pictures, in fashions, in spectacles of all kinds, anything that we can collect or watch—instead of *doing*.

We look for life in the image of life.

TELEVISION

a look behind the 'scenes':
inside the mind of a serial killer

Watching from the Sidelines

The curious thing about a spectacle is how it *immobilizes* the spectators: just like the image, it centers their attention, their values, and ultimately their lives around something outside of themselves. It keeps them occupied without making them active, it keeps them feeling involved without giving them control. You can probably think of a thousand different examples of this: television programs, action movies, magazines that give updates on the lives of celebrities and superstars, spectator sports, representative "democracy," the Catholic church.

A spectacle also isolates the people whose attention it commands. Many of us know more about the fictitious characters of popular sitcoms than we know about the lives and loves of our neighbors—for even when we talk to them, it is about television shows, the news, and the weather; thus the very experiences and information that we share in common as spectators of the mass-media serve to separate us from one another. It is the same at a big football game: everybody watching from the bleachers is a nobody, regardless of who they are. They may be sitting next to each other, but all eyes are focused on the field. If they speak to each other, it is almost never *about* each other, but about the game that is being played before them.

And although football fans cannot participate in the events of the game they are watching, or exert any real influence over them, they attach the utmost importance to these events and associate their own needs and desires with the outcome in a most unusual way. Rather than concentrating their attention on things that have a real bearing on their desires, they reconstruct their desires to revolve around the things they pay attention to. Their language even conflates the achievements of the team they identify themselves with with their own actions: "we scored a goal!" "we won!" shout the fans from their seats and sofas.

This stands in stark contrast to the way people speak about the things that go on in our own cities and communities. "They're building a new highway," we say about the new changes in our neighborhood. "What will they think of next?" we say about the latest advances in scientific technology. Our language reveals that we think of ourselves as spectators in our own societies. But it's not "They," the mysterious Other People, who have made the world the way it is—it is we, humanity ourselves. No small team of scientists, city planners, and rich bureaucrats could have done all the working and inventing and organizing that it has taken for us to transform this planet; it has taken and still takes all of us, working together, to do this. *We* are the ones doing it, every day. And yet most of us seem to feel that we can have more control over football games than we can over our cities, our jobs, even our own lives.

We might have more success in our pursuit of happiness if we start trying to really *participate*. Instead of accepting the role of passive spectator to sports, society, and life, it is up to each of us to figure out how to play an active and significant part in creating the worlds around us and within us. Perhaps one day we can build a new society in which we can all be involved together in the decisions that affect the lives we lead; then we will be able to truly choose our own destinies.

What's the point of doing anything if nobody's watching?

We all want to be famous, to be *seen*, frozen, preserved in the media, because we've come to trust what is *seen* more than what is actually lived. Somehow we've gotten everything backwards and images seem more real to us than experiences. To know that we really exist, that we really matter, we have to see ghosts of ourselves preserved in photographs, on television shows and videotapes, in the public eye.

And when you go on vacation, what do you see? Scores of tourists with video cameras screwed to their faces, as if they're trying to suck all of the real world into the two-dimensional world of images, spending their "time off" seeing the world through a tiny glass lens. Sure, turning everything that you could experience with all five senses into recorded information that you can only observe from a distance, detached, offers you the illusion of having control over your life: you can rewind and replay them, over and over, until everything looks ridiculous. But what kind of life is that?

What's the point of *watching* anything if nobody's *doing?*

ROCK 'N' ROLL

oday not many people know that when the Bill Haley and the Comets song "Rock Around the Clock" was released it caused riots. Young men and women who heard it for the first time on the soundtrack to *The Blackboard Jungle* slashed open seats in theaters, threw soda pop bottles at the screen, and charged out into the streets to kick in windows and

terrorist's manual *Do It!,* young women who had never experienced orgasm before discovered it in record numbers in the wake of concerts by such corporate running dogs as Elvis Presley—it seemed the corporations had finally created a product that could undermine their own power.

But the rock'n'roll fans never developed an analysis of what it was their

overturn cars before the first chorus was even over. For months the suburbs were thick with prowling teenagers, electrified with emotions that were being felt for the first time in generations, knowing that they had to do something—no one knew what—or else it seemed they would explode. As Jerry Rubin noted in his celebrated

music gave them a taste of, and consequently were unable, as a group, to get beyond the threshold of the wild, primal freedom this taste promised. When the first rock'n'roll bands had shown that the unspoken rules governing music were nothing more than illusions, it had made them feel that *all* rules and laws might be mere illusions,

that *anything* might be possible; but because they did not immediately act upon this exhilarating feeling by abolishing all the separations that make hierarchy and capitalism possible in the West, they ended by being reintegrated into the existing system as the alienated producers and consumers of a new series of disembodied products—the paraphernalia of "rebellious youth." As they did not challenge the distinction between artist and society and the division of labor and resources upon which it is founded, they were easily divided and conquered: a few of them became artists, channeling their revolutionary urges into the harmless creation of more (less and less challenging) music—with the permission of the record companies that control access to the means of musical production, of course—while the rest were forced to remain consumers, too busy earning money (which they now needed not only for survival, but also to purchase records) to participate even in this squandering of revolutionary energies, except as spectators.

To this day, rock musicians still seek to reenact the old ritual of liberation through transgression, with occasional success in the most underground of circles; but it seems clear that unless (until?) this can become a part of the total transformation of life, rather than a diversion from it, it will only serve to keep the present system of misery in place. ❀

vandalism committed by youths who have just heard "Rock Around the Clock" for the first time.

☜ GREED ON WALL ST.?
TURN TO PAGE 157

is for Love

Falling in love is the ultimate act of revolution, of *resistance* to today's tedious, socially restrictive, culturally constrictive, patently ridiculous world.

Love transforms the world. Where the lover formerly felt boredom, he now feels passion. Where she once was complacent, she now is excited and compelled to self-asserting action. The world which once seemed empty and tiresome becomes filled with meaning, filled with risks and rewards, with majesty and danger. Life for the lover is a gift, an adventure with the highest possible stakes; every moment is memorable, heartbreaking in its fleeting beauty. When he falls in love, a man who once felt disoriented, alienated, and confused finally knows

Join the Resistance:

Fall in Love

exactly what he wants. Suddenly his existence makes sense to him; it becomes valuable, even glorious and noble. Burning passion is an antidote that will cure the worst cases of despair and resignation.

Love makes it possible for individuals to connect to others in a meaningful way—it impels them to leave their shells and risk being honest and spontaneous together, to come to know each other in profound ways. Thus love makes it possible for us to care about each other genuinely, rather than at the end of the gun of Christian doctrine. But at the same time, it plucks the lover out of the routines of everyday life and separates her from other human beings. She feels a million miles away from the herd of humanity, living as she is in a world entirely different from theirs.

In this sense love is subversive, because it poses a threat to the established order of our modern lives. The boring rituals of workday productivity and socialized etiquette no longer mean anything to a man who has fallen in love, for there are more important forces guiding him than mere inertia and deference to tradition. Marketing strategies that depend upon apathy or insecurity have no effect upon him. Entertainment designed for passive consumption, which depends upon exhaustion or cynicism, can no longer interest him.

There is no place for the passionate, romantic lover in today's world, business or private—for he can see that it might be more worthwhile to hitchhike to Alaska (or to sit in the park and watch the clouds sail by) with his sweetheart than to study for his calculus exam or sell real estate . . . and if he decides that it is, he will have the courage to do it rather than be tormented by unsatisfied longing. He knows that breaking into a cemetery and making love under the stars will make for a more memorable night than watching television ever could. So love poses a threat to our consumer-driven economy, which depends upon consumption of largely useless products and the labor that this consumption necessitates to perpetuate itself.

Similarly, love poses a threat to our political system, for it is difficult to convince a man who has a lot to live for in his personal relationships to be willing to fight and die for an abstraction such as the state; for that matter, it may be difficult to convince him to even pay taxes. It poses a threat to cultures of all kinds, for when human beings are given wisdom and valor by true love they will not be held back by traditions or customs which are irrelevant to the feelings that guide them.

Love even poses a threat to our society itself. Passionate love is ignored and feared by the bourgeoisie, for it poses a great danger to the stability and pretense they covet. Love permits no lies, no falsehoods, not even any polite half-truths, but lays all emotions bare and reveals secrets which domesticated men and women cannot bear. You cannot lie with your emotional and sexual response; situations or ideas excite or repel

If we can resist our passions . . . . . . it is more due to their weakness than our strength.

–Joan of Arc

you
whether
you like it or not,
whether it is polite
or not, whether it is ad-
visable or not. One cannot be a
lover and a dreadfully responsible,
dreadfully respectable member of today's society at the same time;
for love impels you to do things which are not "responsible" or "respectable." True love is irresponsible, irrepressible, rebellious, scorn-
ful of cowardice, dangerous to the lover and everyone around her, for
it serves one master alone: the passion that makes the heart beat faster.
It disdains anything else, be it self-preservation, duty, or shame. Love
urges men and women to heroism, and to antiheroism—to indefen-
sible acts that *need* no defense for the one who loves.

For the lover speaks a different moral and emotional language
than the typical bourgeois man does. The average bourgeois man has
no overwhelming, smoldering desires. Sadly, all he knows is the silent
despair that comes of spending his life pursuing goals set for him by
his family, his educators, his employers, his nation, and his culture,
without ever being able to consider what needs and wants he might

have of his own. Without the burning fire of desire to guide him, he has no criteria upon which to choose what is right and wrong for himself. Consequently he is forced to adopt some dogma or doctrine to direct him through his life. There are a wide variety of moralities to choose from in the marketplace of ideas, but which morality a man buys into is immaterial so long as he chooses one because he is at a loss otherwise as to what he should do with himself and his life. How many men and women, having never realized that they had the option to choose their own destinies, wander through life in a dull haze thinking and acting in accordance with the laws that have been taught to them, merely because they no longer have any other idea what to do? But the lover needs no prefabricated principles to direct her; her desires identify what is right and wrong for her, for her heart guides her through life. She sees beauty and meaning in the world, because her desires paint the world in these colors. She has no need for dogmas, for moral systems, for commandments and imperatives, for she knows what to do without instructions.

Thus she does indeed pose quite a threat to our society. What if *everyone* decided right and wrong for themselves, without any regard for conventional morality? What if *everyone* did whatever they wanted to, with the courage to face any consequences? What if *everyone* feared loveless, lifeless monotony more than they fear taking risks, more than they fear being hungry or cold or in danger? What if *everyone* set down their "responsibilities" and "common sense," and dared to pursue their wildest dreams, to set the stakes high and live each day as if it were the last? Think what a place the world would be! Certainly it would be different than it is now—and it is quite a truism that people from the "mainstream," the simultaneous keepers and victims of the status quo, fear change.

And so, despite the stereotyped images used in the media to sell toothpaste and honeymoon suites, genuine passionate love is discouraged in our culture. Being "carried away by your emotions" is frowned upon; instead we are raised to always be on our guard, lest our hearts lead us astray. Rather than being encouraged to have the courage to face the consequences of risks taken in pursuit of our hearts' desires, we are counseled not to take risks at all, to be "responsible." And love itself is regulated. Men must not fall in love with other men, nor women with other women, nor individuals from different ethnic backgrounds with each other, or else the usual bigots who form the front-line of

fensive in the assault of modern Western culture upon the individual will step in. Men and women who have already entered into a legal/ religious contract are not to fall in love with anyone else, even if they no longer feel any passion for their marital partners. Love as most of us know it today is a carefully prescribed and preordained ritual, something that happens on Friday nights in expensive movie theaters and restaurants, something that fills the pockets of the shareholders in the entertainment industries without preventing workers from showing up to the office on time and ready to reroute phone calls all day long. This regulated, commercial "love" is nothing like the burning fire that consumes the genuine lover. Restrictions, expectations, and regulations smother true love; for love is a wild flower that can never grow within the confines prepared for it, but only appears where it is least expected.

We must fight against these cultural restraints that would cripple and smother our desires. For it is love that gives meaning to life, desire that makes it possible for us to make sense of our existence and find purpose in our lives. Without these, there is no way for us to determine how to live our lives, except to submit to some authority, to some god, master or doctrine that will tell us what to do and how to do it without ever giving us the satisfaction that self-determination does. So fall in love today, with men, with women, with music, with ambition, with yourself . . . with life!

One might say that it is ridiculous to implore others to fall in love—one either falls in love or one does not, it is not a choice that can be made consciously. Emotions do not follow the instructions of the rational mind. But the environment in which we must live out our lives has a great influence on our emotions, and we can make decisions that affect this environment. It should be possible to work to change an environment that is hostile to love into an environment that encourages it. Our task must be to engineer our world so that it is a world in which people can and do fall in love, and thus to reconstitute human beings so that we will be ready for the "revolution" spoken of in these pages—so that we will be able to find meaning and happiness in our lives.

THE CONQUEST OF THE NEW YORK STOCK EXCHANGE

Two old school chums of Eldridge Cleaver turned up at the New York Stock Exchange, their pockets stuffed with one dollar bills. When the doorman tried to deny them entry, accusing them of being "hippies," they protested, in outrage, "We're not hippies, we're *Jews!*" and he didn't dare refuse them.

They walked out onto the balcony that overlooks the stock market itself, and began throwing bills over the railing to the stockbrokers below. The stockbrokers all dropped what they were doing and ran around pushing and leaping after the bills until the police came to drag the two "hippies" away. As a result of the interruption in their workday, the entire market crashed that day and all the stockbrokers and stockholders lost thousands of dollars. The whole thing was caught by television cameras, and that night families across the U.S. were treated to images of businessmen revealing their true natures of pathological, fetishist greed. A few weeks later, bulletproof glass and a thick metal grate were installed between the viewer's balcony and the exchange floor, and the doormen were instructed not to permit Jews to enter. ✾

COSTUME/STREET PARTY ON PAGE 166

is for their Media, Movement, and Myth

Working "Within the System"
If you beat them at their own game, you've lost.

So . . . you're in a band, with a really important message, and you want to get it out to as many people as possible—so you're trying to get really popular and sell lots and lots of records. Or perhaps you're a political activist and you think it's necessary to use the mainstream media to educate people about certain issues. It seems to make sense that you should use these methods to reach people—because otherwise, who will notice you? Yes, you realize that you're making compromises with the very system you're trying to fight, but it'll be worth it in the end . . . and we all have to make compromises, don't we?

It's worth considering whether we do after all, just as it's worth questioning whether getting ahead in their system of cutthroat competition and mass-marketing can ever really help us change the world. What would happen if we stopped compromising, stopped playing their game altogether and concentrated all our efforts on creating channels of our own for spreading ideas in new ways?

The Revolution Cannot Be Televised.

"On stage I make love to ten thousand people, then I go home alone."

–Janis Joplin

Of course they want you on their television show, radio program, rock festival, major label. They don't care whether they're selling mouthwash or anarchist revolution as long as they can keep people watching and buying. They know that sooner or later people are bound to get bored and fed up with the mindless, passionless drivel that they normally have to offer, and they count on you to keep new ideas and styles coming for them to exploit; without that, they'd have nothing new to sell people. They know if they can find ways to sell your own expressions of outrage back to you, to cash in on the very frustration that their system creates, they've got you beat. They know that no message you could spread through their channels could be more powerful than the message that your use of their medium itself sends: *stay tuned.*

No awareness you could possibly raise with television appearances or CDs sold in shopping malls is more important than the awareness of the power of individuals to act for themselves. Television watching and supermarket shopping keep people passive, watching things that they can never take part in and people they can never meet, buying what is marketed to them by corporations rather than making their own music, their own ideas, their own lives. To motivate people to act for themselves, you have to contact them more directly.

The Values of Mass Production.

We're taught to think of our success in terms of numbers, aren't we? If touching one person's life is a good thing, then touching one thousand people's lives must be a great thing. It's easy to see where we learned to think this way: our whole society revolves around mass production. The more units we can move, the more customers we can serve, the more votes we can get, the more money and stuff we have, the better, right?

But maybe it's not possible to touch a thousand people as deeply or as powerfully as one person or ten people. And maybe it's not really so revolutionary after all to have one person or group telling everybody else what's right. Wouldn't it be better to try a decentralized approach where everyone works closely with those around them, instead of a few people leading an anonymous mass? Do you, or your band, or your label have to save the world all by yourselves? Why don't you trust anyone else to do it with you? (And have you noticed how much you have to stomp all over everyone else to get that success you plan to use to spread your message?)

One political band playing a show to nine hundred people can recite revolutionary slogans for everyone present to stand and listen to, but they remain out of arm's reach of most of the people there, up on a pedestal as "musicians," "artists," "heroes." On the other hand, one band playing an equally impassioned show to forty people, in a more intimate setting, can interact on a personal level with everyone there, and make it clear that everyone is capable of doing what they do. Thus they have the potential to spark four more bands (or similar revolutionary projects), increasing their impact exponentially. The same goes for record labels, for writers, for speakers and artists, and of course for organizers and "leaders" of any kind.

Working Within the System.

Most of us don't get much pleasure out of the things we have to do to work inside the system. We'd rather be reading books on our own than writing assigned papers for school, rather be using our skills, energy, and time to work on projects of our own choice than selling ourselves to employers. But we feel like we *have* to work for them, whether we like it or not. It never occurs to us how much more fun, and perhaps more effective, it could be to take our labor out of their hands and do something else with it. *Sure* it would be hard at first, but

SON, REVOLUTION IS NOT SHOWING LIFE TO PEOPLE, BUT MAKING THEM LIVE.

what could be harder than to have to put up with this bullshit for the rest of our lives? Better we dedicate ourselves to replacing it than just dealing with it.

But, you protest, you're still going to be fighting the status quo, you're going to change things from the inside, right? That's what *they* tell you, at least. Of course the system has "appropriate procedures" for people with grievances to go through to try to make things better; that's the safety valve to release pressure when people get *too* worked up. Do you think the powers that be would really let anyone use their own laws and methods to depose them? If this system provided opportunities for real change, people would have taken advantage of them a long time ago. Countless generations have set out convinced that they would succeed where other had failed—that's where lawyers and reporters *come from,* you know. They're the cynical corpses of idealistic young men and women who thought the system could be reformed.

Besides, can you trust yourself to work "within the system" for the right reasons? We're all programmed to want "success," to measure ourselves by wealth and social status, whether we like it or not. Could it be that you want to become a journalist or professor of political science or rock star because you can't bring yourself to consider

any other options seriously, because you're afraid to try cutting to the safety line that ties you to the security of a mainstream lifestyle? And how can you be sure it isn't that dark corner of your heart pushing you to seek success, the part that loves the attention and feelings of greatness your popularity and social standing bring? Sure it feels great to be able to tell your parents what your goals are and have them applaud your decisions . . . but is that any way to decide how to go about changing the world?

Let's listen to our hearts, trust our instincts, and refuse to participate in anything that bores or outrages us. We need to nourish our idealism and our willingness to take risks, not work out new ways to integrate our frustration and our desperation for change back into the society that engendered them. Remember, every day we spend "using the system" is another day longer we'll have to wait until new networks and better ways of life replace the old ones.

How do we get out of here?

Yes, it often seems like there's no alternative to working "within the system" if we want to get things done and not keep our ideas quarantined within the narrow confines of the underground. But why keep the underground quarantined to narrow confines? Surely if we put all our energy into expanding the spaces in which we can interact as free, equal human beings, rather than trying to repair the burning machinery of this doomed society, we could make at least as much of an impact. Imagine what we could achieve if we kept all our potential in our own hands, and refused to waste it ever again working for their system for even a minute.

There's no excuse to let a fraction of our lives go by doing things we don't love, or to let any of our talents and efforts serve to prop up a world order we oppose. Instead, let's fight so hard, and live so hard, that others inside the cages of mainstream life can see us and are inspired to join us in our complete rejection of the old world and all its bullshit. And let's make our communities something greater than they are; let's make them more open and more capable of offering life-support, so that others really will be able to join us.

The system we live under offers only losers' games—so why play them? It's up to us to create new games, more joyous and exciting than the old ones. Let's not try to beat them at their games, but make them join us in ours!

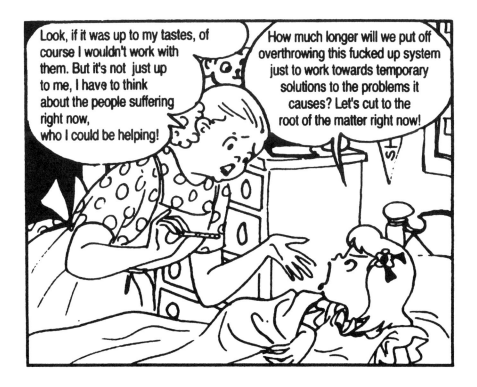

THE PARIS COMMUNE RETURNS FROM THE DEAD

A full-scale revolution broke out in France (which, in fact, was one of the few Western nations in which rock music was not yet popular with the young), starting as a public uproar over the harsh treatment of a handful of students who had taken advantage of student apathy to get themselves elected to class council in order to "misappropriate" school funding for the purpose of printing subversive literature. Thousands of students and workers took to the streets in protest, and ended up fighting the police for those streets, which they won from them and held for almost a month. The entire working class went on strike and

restored, and the illusion of docile satisfaction with it; and until today, the forces that pushed France to the edge of total social transformation have remained hidden, dormant.

The Situationist International, a body of ultra-radical theorists and ex-artists, is often cited as having the most lucid account of what the revolution of May 1968 was about. The ideas and actions of the S.I. are certainly an important part of the ancestry of the CrimethInc. collective, but we're not going to write about them here. They've been discussed and analyzed enough already by careerist culture-industry commentators who, knowingly or not,

occupied their workplaces in solidarity; the universities were taken over and people of all walks of life gathered there around the clock to discuss and debate what the new world should be. At the last moment, after the revolutionary occupation councils had already sent out telegrams to all the governments of the world (and the Pope, too) announcing that the last hours of their barbaric reigns were at hand, the labor unions and left wing parties sabotaged the whole thing by ordering those who still trusted them back to work in return for a small increase in wages. "Order" was

have endeavored to undermine their efforts to change the world by presenting them as mere history (and thus, in the case of said careerists, just another subject to research—for profit). The real way to pay them homage is to *do* what they were doing, stealing their ideas to use where appropriate, rather than contemplating them as a part of what they would have decried as the Spectacle of History (i.e., the history of the Spectacle). ✤

☞ *NEW WAYS TO ESCAPE FROM JAIL ON PAGE 173*

Dear CrimethInc. folks:

So, you've got all these great ideas here—why are you wasting them on the deaf ears of punk rockers and other latecomers to dead radicalisms? Shouldn't you be trying to form a new movement of your own, Crimethinkism, just like the communists and the nudists did?

I. Nietzsche's Answer: No.

A Movement is based on an ideological construct: not a convergence of unique desires, but a standard for what those desires should be—or, at best, a set model for how to integrate different desires. As such, Movement as a concept has the same relationship to the life we seek as the Image does to lived experience: it is an inorganic representation of an organic thing. You can't trap the joys of feeling free and generous and alive in any social construct, be it the Adventurists International or the Maoist Boy Scouts, any more than you can render passion permanent in a love relationship by getting married. The adventures and sensations we seek are wild animals, and they won't

hold still in the social conventions of any movement, not even for us.

   This is not to say that forming free associations in pursuit of our goals is always self-defeating—quite the contrary!—but we must be wary, lest our groups become Movements. Just as images divert attention from the necessarily invisible things that are truly valuable (e.g., the boy who sees a powerful performance by an anarchist theater troupe, and associates the feeling of liberation they evoked in him with their extravagant clothing), so do Movements trap us in the trappings—*any* trappings, whether theoretical (ideology) or practical (organizational structure, tradition, etc.)—of our real quest, which is for Life itself. It shouldn't be hard for the resourceful reader to come up with examples of movements that have begun by channeling vital forces and ended as pathetic parodies of them: for politics, the Communist Party; for the arts, surrealism, or jazz, or "emo" hardcore; for culture, the hippies, the beatniks, the punks.

   Guy Debord dissolved the Situationist International, an organization partly responsible for the near-successful French revolution of 1968, shortly after that uprising: when people began trying to join in order to be associated with such a prestigious radical group, rather than because they thought there was something new they could contribute to it. He explained that he did so to prevent the S.I. from becoming a Movement in the sense described above—thus their legacy could retain its charge, to be used like a bomb by future generations.[6] This stands as a good example of how we can protect ourselves by keeping ahead of the accumulating inertia of our own endeavors.

With images and movements, it is better to remain fleet of foot: to shift unexpectedly, subverting expectations, perhaps flirting playfully with one image or another (as it is impossible to have *no* image: everything looks like *something*), but never trusting or committing. And it may be that a good strategy to avoid the stultifying effects of becoming a Movement, and the dangerous attentions of careerist historicizers (like Greil Marcus), is to do our work within supposedly "dead" movements, like punk rock. By doing so, we emphasize two truths that cannot be emphasized enough: that the Life and Freedom we seek can pop up anywhere, unexpected, unpredictable—if that's not the case, we really are in trouble—and that there never *could* be a Movement centering around Life itself, since it can be found *anywhere,* but expected nowhere.

II. Nadia's Answer: Absolutely Not.

If history is the *chain* of events—the causal, determinist replication of a world in which everything is predictable (or would be, if you had enough information) and the magic of total freedom is impossible—and our revolutionary myths refer to that other, supernatural world, the one that our dreams and desires describe (a world that manifests itself only through transcendent music and similar miracles: phenomena that evoke beauty and meaning without being rationally explicable)—then what we are really looking for are loopholes *out* of history and into that other world. Such loopholes appear every once in a while; the greatest of our myths, of course, is that we can some-

---

[6] Too bad that now, thanks to the avaricious efforts of paid cultural critics like Greil "Herbert" Marcus (author of *Undimensional Man* and *Zeros in Civilization*), they've finally been made a part of History, set in the past and thus rendered inorganic—now slogans that once were inspiring and dangerous in our plagiarists' hands are merely *dated,* and the plagiarism that was creative action is now mere repetition.

how pass their event horizon to escape *forever* from history into the ahistorical space of total freedom.

A movement is an *historical* force: an attempt to act *within* the chain of events to shift its direction. Such efforts have succeeded in the past, but such success is not what we want. What we want is something that, by its very nature, has never happened before: to break the chain of events that binds us, to bring history to an end, so that an entirely new world can begin. For this to be possible, we'll need the perfect convergence of *ahistorical* forces.

This is not something that can be arranged by any efforts inside the flow of history; it is not something that can be arranged at all, really, but only believed in, as we keep striking matches and tossing them out until one ignites the final fire. Total revolution will not come merely as the result of proper planning and hard work (this isn't wage labor, you know!), but out of a leap of faith: faith in the boundless possibilities of what today appears a sterile and predictable world. Like everything grand or awful in life, it cannot be earned or deserved; rejecting the assumptions of exchange economy thinking (that everything has an exchange value, and even revolution can be bought with a certain amount of blood and sweat) will help to clarify this. We could work around the clock for the rest of eternity, meticulously constructing and deploying strategy after strategy, without coming any closer to real revolution (even if we achieved a few botched counterfeits, like the Russian or Chinese examples); or, just as possibly, one thoughtlessly defiant creative act at the right moment might be all it takes to start the chain reaction we've dreamed of for so long.

Lest this all sound like anarcho-mystical academic nonsense (which it *is*, of course—freedom cannot be understood except through mysticism!), here's a concrete (historical!) example. The brief "adolescent wildness" of students, which has traditionally served to appease and squander their libertine impulses and rebellions in preparation for miserable adulthood, has always been an historical force—a tendency easily explained in terms of social conditions, which also serves to maintain them; but, at the same time, it has sometimes coexisted with an ahistorical force: those rare sensations of real freedom and weightlessness that youth and student life sometimes create, a phenomenon that cannot truly be described or explained in terms of history or cause and effect, that sociologists might refer to from afar but never actually comprehend. The Situationist International, which NietzsChe mentions above, did not set out to create a movement among rebellious students; such a thing, even if it had succeeded in altering the details of their alienation, would never have been able to spring them out of the history (of academia, youth rebellion, Western Civilization and lifelessness in general, etc.) in which they were trapped. Instead, the Situationists were faithful to their own desires for a world grander than anything that could proceed from the historical trends of their time, and set out to discover and empower other ahistorical forces concealed in the world around them; to accomplish this, they attempted to create tools of theory and analysis which could be used to drill an escape route right out of the long night of capitalist history. It was the fortuitous encounter of the analytical tools they created with the ahistorical fancies of a mere handful of adventurous students at Strasbourg that unleashed the flood of unchecked desire which nearly transformed the whole world.[7]

Read all this as a metaphor if you must, or merely as a new way to interpret history (for *everything* is history to some of you, casualties of a world that no longer admits to anything magical); but *that* is how real revolution happens. To get to it, we don't need the most flawlessly constructed plans, the most fastidiously organized movements, or the most carefully designed systems; rather, each of us must be faithful to the yearnings of her heart for things too extravagant to ever fit in this world, and pursue them to such lengths that others are inspired to their own pursuits. It is this alchemy we need, not another movement.

---

[7] It's also important to point out that all the existing movements in France at that time, including the most supposedly radical (the Communist Party, the labor unions, etc.), opposed the insurrection from its very beginning until its final defeat at their hands; those who had spent decades trying to work within the flow of history, investing themselves in it, were not ready to watch it end and 'let their people go,' in the words of the old spiritual. And though the grassroots structures of some of the labor unions helped to facilitate the organizing of the new Workers' Councils, they only were of use because they were not being used for their intended purpose; thus the alchemy metaphor offers itself to us as a way to represent the question of how to transform existing structures and resources into the raw materials of a totally *new* world.

THE GERMAN COURTROOM GETAWAY

Without guns, hacksaws, or hostages, three German radicals managed to liberate one of their number from the clutches of the "justice" system in the middle of a court hearing. The three were on trial for various charges (including arson and assault) resulting from their activism against the capitalist/military establishment. Two of them, Michael "Bommi" Baumann and Thomas Weisbecker, were expecting to be released on parole, while the third, Georg von Rauch, was going to be sentenced to at least ten years in prison, when the court adjourned for an afternoon break. Thomas and Georg both had long hair and beards, and looked quite similar to each other in the unsophisticated eyes of the police and lawyers; so before reentering the courtroom, Georg gave his spectacles to Thomas. When Thomas and Bommi were given parole and declared free to leave, Bommi and Georg leaped up and made quite a commotion, hugging and shaking hands with everyone and shouting. Both then quickly exited the building and disappeared, leaving Thomas, whom everyone had assumed was Georg. When the marshal came to lead Thomas away in chains, he protested that he had just been released on parole and the frustrated guards had to let him go, too.

Following the escape, the three form a new guerrilla organization, the June 2nd Movement, named for the day in 1967 when an unarmed student radical was murdered by a policeman during a demonstration. Georg himself was shot to death by police five months later, followed after another three months by Thomas, but the J2M went on to finance plenty of underground work through bank robberies and pulled off such incredible stunts as the kidnapping of politician Peter Lorenz, who

was successfully exchanged for five imprisoned political prisoners in 1975. Bommi moved on from terrorism to other underground activities, including writing an account of his experiences as a guerrilla, entitled *How It All Began.* Upon the book's publication, the German government suspended freedom of speech nationally in order to confiscate and destroy all copies, just as it sidestepped the so-called justice system two years later to murder three political prisoners from the R.A.F. (a companion group of the J2M) in their cells.[4]

---

[4] Of course, if you'd like to read this book, just contact your nearest CrimethInc. branch office.

☞ *THE BIRTH OF VENGEANCE ON PAGE 176*

Myth.

Dearest Nadia,

I've read some of the manuscript, as you asked. Listen, tell me: all these myths—revolution, the complete destruction of hierarchy, the union of self-interest with generosity, perfect freedom as permanent liberation from every bond including the laws of nature—are they intended to represent attainable goals, or are they just symbols to pursue as they recede before us?

My dear E—,

Well, the latter, obviously, to guide us and give us something to aim for beyond the absurdities of our present condition. But also—if we believe, as the heretics of the Free Spirit did, that heaven is attainable on earth, that the barrier between the natural (the world as it seems to be, history as a series of predictable reactions, as a *chain* of events) and the supernatural (our passions, our desires for things outside *this* world, which are invisible to history, which our songs and daydreams refer to) can be magically dissolved—and some of us do!—then yes, take these myths literally, too. We are madwomen and madmen, the mad holy men of the new age, who are maniacs for still believing in *anything* in this nihilistic day. So be it!

Yes, what we want is something that has never happened before—by its very nature! So we can't look backwards for precedents, only look forward to try to make this wild dream a reality once and for all. No one has ever tried this before—that's why it's going to work.

And that's why myths, as intimations of what could be, are so much more powerful than facts today—even though (no, *because*) they may not be based on things that are "objectively true" of the world right now. CrimethInc. itself is mostly a myth right now—but a myth that has *power*, because it points towards a world most of us want more than this one. I dare you, if it's something *you* want, to make it come true.

CRIMETHINC. IS BORN

According to one legend, CrimethInc. began on a sunny morning in May when a future CrimethInc. worker (name withheld to protect the guilty) picked up hitchhiker Nadia C. on his way to work. The two found themselves in a conversation so intense that he drove right past his workplace and out into the country, where they took a long walk and continued talking. At the end of the walk he called his boss on his cellular phone, told him he quit, and then threw the phone into the lake by the side of the road. In the spirit of the moment the two decided to start a revolutionary organization then and there.

CrimethInc. cabalists interpret the story as an allegory representing the union of the oppressed working class with the bohemian/radical resistance, but Nadia insists that it did actually happen.

☞ *WHAT THE FUCK SHOULD THIS SAY ON PAGE 186*

*is for Plagiarism,
Politics, and
Production*

PLAGIARISM.

A CRIMETHINC. EXCLUSIVE!

(CON-)TEXT AND IDEAS SEIZED AND REDEPLOYED
BY TRISTRAN TZARATHUSTRA AND STELLA NERA.

I. "Intellectual Property"

We have all been taught from our youth that there is nothing new under the sun. Whenever a child has an exciting idea, an older person is quick to point out either that this idea has been tried before and didn't work, or that someone else not only has already had the idea but also has developed and expounded upon it to greater lengths than the child ever could. "Learn and choose from the ideas and beliefs already in circulation, rather than seeking to develop and arrange your own," is the message, and this message is sent clearly by the methods of instruction used in both public and private schools throughout the West.

Despite this common attitude, or perhaps because of it, we are very possessive of our ideas. The concept of intellectual property is ingrained in the collective psychosis even deeper than the concept of material property. Plenty of thinkers have asserted that "property is theft"[8] in regard to real estate and other physical capital, but few have dared to make similar statements about their own ideas. Even the most notoriously "radical" thinkers have still proudly claimed their ideas as, first and foremost, *their* ideas.

Consequently, little distinction is made between thinkers and their thoughts. Students of philosophy will study the philosophy of Descartes, students of economics will study Marx-ism, students of art will study the paintings of Dali. At worst, the cult of personality that develops around famous thinkers prevents any useful consideration of their ideas or artwork; hero-worshipping partisans will swear allegiance to a thinker and all his thoughts, while others who have some objection to the "owner" of the ideas have a hard time not being prejudiced against the ideas themselves. At best, this emphasis upon the "author-owner" in the consideration of propositions or artwork is merely irrelevant to the worth of the actual propositions or artwork, even if the stories about the individual in question are interesting and can encourage creative thinking by themselves.

The very assumptions behind the concept of "intellectual property" require more attention than we have given them. The factors that affect the words and deeds of an individual are many and varied, not the least of them being her social-cultural climate and the input of other individuals. To say that any idea has its sole origins in the being of one individual man or woman is to grossly oversimplify. But

---

[8]This is actually a problematic assertion, since the judgment "theft is wrong" depends upon the assumption "respecting property is right."

we are so accustomed to claiming items and objects for ourselves, and to being forced to accept similar claims from others, in the cutthroat competition that is life in a market economy, that it seems natural to do the same with ideas. Certainly there must be other ways of thinking about the origins and ownership of ideas . . . for our present approach does more than merely distract from the ideas themselves.

Our tradition of recognizing "intellectual property rights" is dangerous in that it results in the deification of the publicly recognized "thinker" and "artist" at the expense of everyone else. When ideas are always associated with proper names (and always the *same* proper names), this suggests that thinking and creating are special skills that belong to a select few individuals. For example, the glorification of the "artist" in our culture, which includes the stereotyping of artists as eccentric "visionaries" who exist at the edge (the "avant garde") of society, encourages people to believe that artists are significantly and fundamentally different from other human beings. Actually, anyone can be an artist, and everyone is, to some extent. But when we are led to believe that being creative and thinking critically are talents which only a few individuals possess, those of us who are not fortunate enough to be christened "artists" or "philosophers" by our communities will not make much effort to develop these abilities. Consequently we are dependent upon others for many of our ideas, and must be content as spectators of their creative work.

Another incidental drawback of our association of ideas with specific individuals is that it promotes the acceptance of these ideas in their original form. The students who learn the philosophy of Descartes are encouraged to learn it in its orthodox form, rather than learning the parts which they find relevant to their own lives and interests and combining these parts with ideas from other sources. Out of deference to the original thinker, deified as he is in our tradition, his texts and theories are to be preserved as-is, without ever being put into new forms or contexts which might reveal new insights. Mummified as they are, many theories become completely irrelevant to modern existence, when they could have been given a new lease on life by being treated with a little less reverence.

So we can see that our acceptance of the tradition of "intellectual property" has negative effects upon our endeavors to think critically and learn from our artistic and philosophical heritage. What can we do to address this problem?

One of the possible solutions is plagiarism.

II. Plagiarism and the Modern Revolutionary

Plagiarism is an especially effective method of appropriating and reorganizing ideas, and as such it can be a useful tool for a young man or woman looking to encourage new and exciting thinking in others. And it is a method that is revolutionary in that it does not recognize "intellectual property" rights but rather strikes out against them and all of the negative effects that recognizing them can have.

Plagiarism focuses attention on content and away from incidental issues, by making the genuine origins of the material impossible to ascertain. Besides, as suggested above, it could be argued that the *genuine* origins of most inspirations and propositions are impossible to determine anyway. By signing a new name, or no name at all, to a text, the plagiarizer puts the material in an entirely new context, and this may generate new perspectives and new thinking about the subject. Plagiarism also makes it possible to combine the best or most relevant parts of a number of texts, thus creating a new text with many of the virtues of the older ones—and some new virtues, as well, since the combination of material from different sources is bound to result in unforeseeable effects, and might well unlock hidden meanings or possibilities that have been dormant in the texts for years. Finally, above all, plagiarism is the reappropriation of ideas: when an individual plagiarizes a text which those who believe in intellectual property would have held "sacred," she denies that there is a difference in rank between herself and the thinker she takes from. She takes the thinker's ideas for herself, to express as she sees fit, rather than treating the thinker as an *authority* whose work she is duty-bound to preserve as he intended. She denies, in fact, that there is a fundamental difference between the thinker and the rest of humanity, by appropriating the thinker's material as the *property* of humanity.

After all, a good idea should be available to everyone—should *belong* to everyone—if it really is a good idea. In a society organized with human happiness as the objective, copyright infringement laws and similar restrictions would not hinder the distribution and recombination of ideas. These impediments only make it more difficult for individuals who are looking for challenging and inspiring material to come upon it and share it with others.

So, if there truly is "nothing new under the sun," take them at their word, and act accordingly. Take what seems relevant to your life and your needs from the theories and doctrines of those who came before you. Don't be afraid to reproduce word for word those texts which seem perfect to you, so you can share them with others who might also benefit from them. And at the same time, don't be afraid

to plunder ideas from different sources and rearrange them in ways that you find more useful and exciting, more relevant to your own needs and experiences. You can create a personalized body of critical and creative thought, with elements gathered from a variety of sources, rather than just choosing from one of the prefabricated ideologies that are offered to you. After all, do we have ideas, or do they have us?

III. Language and the Question of Authorship Itself

Words, musical and artistic conventions, symbols and gestures, all these things are useful only because we hold them in common—that alone makes them currency for communication. Human beings, just like everything else in the world, are not isolated entities: each of us exists as part of a vast web, as an intersection of strands that proceed from every direction. None of us could be what we are if not for the others around us and before us, and the natural world beyond—our thoughts are constructed from the languages spoken around us, our values and narratives are assembled from the found objects of this world; we represent our experiences and memories to ourselves in the configurations developed by the civilization that raised us.

This is not to say that nothing is original; rather, *everything* is original, for every expression, every action, however frequently repeated, issues from a unique point in the web of human relations. But at the same time, this means that the recontextualization of pre-existing elements (which some call "plagiarism") is essential to *all* communication. And if every expression is both borrowed and unique, it seems absurd to try to separate expressions into one category or the other. Yes, each of us participates in the continuation and evolution of the languages we speak; but in truth, the line between imitation and innovation is so blurry that any distinctions are bound to be arbitrary.

If that is the case, then let us leave it to the scientists to figure out the chronological details of who was the first to arrange words or musical notes in a particular order. Much more important, for us, is what we can *do* with these combinations of shared elements.

Some claim for themselves the rights of ownership over combinations they believe (rightly or not) they were the first to apply; many of them justify this by insisting that these combinations are the perfect expression of their emotions or experiences, and that those who read or hear them are being granted direct access to their souls. But the fact is, a poem or song always has a different significance for the listener or reader than it did for the composer. The reader applies the words to her own experiences, searches her heart to see which ones will resonate with the unique emotions she has felt. Like it or not, once you create something and send it out into the world, it has a life of its own in the reactions and emotions it provokes in others—and it will not answer to you or represent you except by coincidence. For the writer, the true significance of the work is in the act of creation itself, in the rearranging and shaping of forms. Those who hope to retain control of the products of their creation afterwards are living in denial.

Thus we can throw out all the superstitions surrounding the author's signature—the question of so-called authenticity, the glorification of self-expression, the concept of intellectual property—and see the signature for what it really is: another element of the composition itself. The signing of a work is a part of the creative process: it offers a context in which the work will be interpreted. What signature could truly capture the complete origins of a work, anyway, considering all the disparate and ancient components that make up any given work of art, and all the human relations and innovations that were necessary to arrive at them? For that matter, if the notion of the fixed, distinct identity of individuals is also a superstition, that ren-

Bad artists imitate.

Great artists steal.

–Pablo Picasso

ders even the *possibility* of an individual signature preposterous! If one wanted to be honest, one would sign the name of one's entire civilization to one's poetry or pottery, and add to that the seal of the cosmos from which it arose—effectively communalizing the work.

This being the case, if the signature is just another element of the composition, it makes just as much sense to sign with another's name, or with a false name (complete perhaps with a fabricated identity), depending on which can offer the context that will best enhance the content of the work. For once we are through with the delusion that we can own expressions, we can focus on the real question of how to create expressions—context and all—that will best serve to help us find ourselves and each other . . . and, then, to transform what we find.

Disclaimer: *All this extolling of artistic theft is* not *meant to be taken as an endorsement of mere repetition. Young would-be plagiarists sometimes miss the point of re-contextualization entirely, and think that it is enough just to parrot what those around them say. But you're not likely to say* anything *true or important like that, are you?*

THE FIRST INTERNATIONAL CRIMETHINC. CONVENTION

The details of the meeting of the first CrimethInc. International (CrimeIntern) are shrouded in myth and fable. Some say the delegates met by chance, trying to scam food from the same restaurant; others claim they gathered at the swimming pool of an expensive hotel, which they had all sneaked into, while still others insist it was just a conversation between an employee of a printing corporation and a CrimethInc. worker who was ripping off free copies with her assistance. Regardless of what the circumstances of the convention actually were, it is universally agreed that it was at this event that the initial tenets of the CrimethInc. party program were established:

Never Work

Don't allow yourself to be bought. Do what you want to do most, not just what you are paid to do. If you sell your time away for money, doing something that is not in itself rewarding for you,
you are selling your life away. What could you possibly buy with that money that would be worth the life you have lost?

There is a difference between life and mere survival. The capitalist economy would sell you mere survival at the cost of your life: it does this by making you spend your life working towards other peoples' goals rather than your own, in order to earn the money to buy things that their advertisements and media have brainwashed you into believing you need.

We each have only a short time on this planet to live and find happiness. Is the life you are living the one which will bring you the most happiness? Are you doing what you do because you love it, or for some other reason? What could possibly justify not doing what you really want to do with your life? To the best of your ability, never work for companies or any other outside forces; do what you do in your life for **yourself.**

Never Rest

Decide what it is you want in life and go for it! Don't just sit around waiting for it to come to you; it probably won't. If you want anything, anything at all, you are going to have to pursue it. It's up to you to figure out how... and to **do** it.

Today we are conditioned to sit still when we are not obeying orders. When we are not at work, we are supposed to sit quietly in front of the television absorbing whatever is fed to us, or to act out predetermined (and absolutely harmless) roles as sports or music fans. But if we are to find happiness in this world, we must learn how to act for ourselves again. We must fight to find new ways of survival and of life, especially if we are to break free of the burdens of "work." We cannot just sit around doing what we are told, going around in the circles of so-called entertainment and "leisure time"; we must invent our own activities, we must motivate ourselves and never rest in our struggle to take our lives back. It's not going to be easy, but it's worth it if anything is!

Raise the Stakes

If a little bit of freedom is a good thing, then a lot of freedom is a great thing. If a little bit of pleasure is nice, then a lot of pleasure is glorious. We are not content to settle for whatever scraps of self-determination and joy come our way under the system that prescribes our lives today. We want everything. We want complete control over every aspect of our lives; we want to taste the sweetest happiness and the most exhilarating liberty this existence has to offer; we want to lead lives that are as heroic, as magnificent as any we could read about in books. We want high stakes: we don't want to just let our lives pass by us, mediocre and tiresome, as so many others have before us.

For this, we are willing to risk anything; for this, we are willing to fight!

All who were present were profoundly moved by the idea of no longer compromising their desires and their time, and spread across the world in all directions to attempt the experiment of living without concessions. ☾

NATURAL BORN PRANKSTERS ON PAGE 193

by Nadia C.

You know it's true. Otherwise, why does everyone cringe when you say the word? Why has attendance at your anarcho-communist theory discussion group meetings fallen to an all-time low? Why has the oppressed proletariat not come to its senses and joined you in your fight for world liberation?

Perhaps, after years of struggling to educate them about their victimhood, you have come to blame them for their condition. They must *want* to be ground under the heel of capitalist imperialism; otherwise, why do they show no interest in your political causes? Why haven't they joined you yet in chaining yourself to mahogany furniture, chanting slogans at carefully planned and orchestrated protests, and frequenting anarchist bookshops? Why haven't they sat down and learned all the terminology necessary for a genuine understanding of the complexities of Marxist economic theory?

The truth is, your politics are boring to them because they really are irrelevant. They know that your antiquated styles of protest—your marches, hand held signs, and gatherings—are now powerless to effect real change because they have become such a predictable part of the status quo. They know that your post-Marxist jargon is off-putting because it really is a language of mere academic dispute, not a weapon capable of undermining systems of control. They know that your infighting, your splinter groups and endless quarrels over ephemeral theories can never effect any real change in the world they experience from day to day. They know that no matter who is in office, what laws are on the books, what "ism"s the intellectuals march under, the content of their lives will remain the same. They—we—know that our boredom is proof that these "politics" are not the key to any real transformation of life. For our lives are boring enough already!

And you know it too. For how many of you is politics a *responsibility*? Something you engage in because you feel you *should*, when in your heart of hearts there are a million things you would rather be doing? Your volunteer work—is it your most favorite pastime, or do you do it out of a sense of obligation? Why do you think it is so hard to motivate others to volunteer as you do? Could it be that it is, above all, a feeling of *guilt* that drives you to fulfill your "duty" to be politically active? Perhaps you spice up your "work" by trying (consciously or not) to get in trouble with the authorities, to get arrested: not because it will practically serve your cause, but to make things more exciting, to recapture a little of the romance of turbulent times now long past. Have you ever felt that you were participating in a ritual, a long-established tradition of fringe protest, that really serves only to strengthen the position of the mainstream? Have you ever secretly longed to escape from the stagnation and boredom of your political "responsibilities"?

It's no wonder that no one has joined you in your political endeavors. Perhaps you tell yourself that it's tough, thankless work, but somebody's got to do it. The answer is, well, NO.

You actually do us all a real disservice with your tiresome, tedious politics. For in fact, there is nothing more important than politics. NOT the politics of American "democracy" and law, of who is elected state legislator to sign the same bills and perpetuate the same system. Not the politics of the *"I got involved with the radical left because I enjoy quibbling over trivial details and writing rhetorically about an unreachable utopia"* anarchist. Not the politics of any leader or ideology that demands that you make sacrifices for "the cause." But the politics of our everyday lives.

When you separate politics from the immediate, everyday experiences of individual men and women, it becomes completely irrelevant. Indeed, it becomes the private domain of wealthy, comfortable intellectuals, who can trouble themselves with such dreary, theoretical things. When you involve yourself in politics out of a sense of obligation, and make political action into a dull responsibility rather than an exciting game that is worthwhile for its own sake, you scare away people whose lives are already far too dull for any more tedium. When you make politics into a lifeless thing, a joyless thing, a dreadful responsibility, it becomes

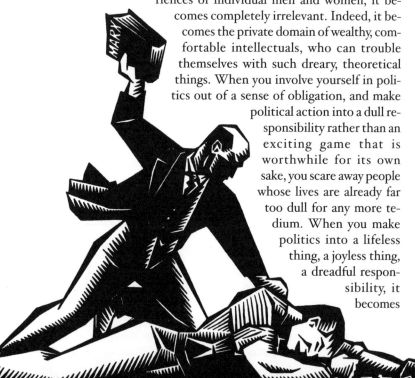

just another weight upon people, rather than a means to lift weight from people. And thus you ruin the idea of politics for the people to whom it should be most important. For everyone has a stake in considering their lives, in asking themselves what they want out of life and how they can get it. But you make politics look to them like a miserable, self-referential, pointless middle class/bohemian game, a game with no relevance to the real lives they are living out.

What should be political? Whether we enjoy what we do to get food and shelter. Whether we feel like our daily interactions with our friends, neighbors, and coworkers are fulfilling. Whether we have the opportunity to live each day the way we desire to. And "politics" should consist not of merely *discussing* these questions, but of acting directly to improve our lives in the immediate present. Acting in a way that is itself entertaining, exciting, joyous—because political action that is tedious, tiresome, and oppressive can only perpetuate tedium, fatigue, and oppression in our lives. No more time should be wasted debating over issues that will be irrelevant when we must go to work again the next day. No more predictable ritual protests that the authorities know all too well how to deal with; no more boring ritual protests which will not sound like a thrilling way to spend a Saturday afternoon to potential volunteers—clearly, those won't get us anywhere. Never again shall we "sacrifice ourselves for the cause." For we *ourselves*, happiness in our own lives and the lives of our fellows, must be our cause!

After we make politics relevant and exciting, the rest will follow. But from a dreary, merely theoretical and/or ritualized politics, nothing valuable can follow. This is not to say that we should show no interest in the welfare of humans, animals, or ecosystems that do not contact us directly in our day to day existence. But the foundation of our politics must be concrete: it must be immediate, it must be obvious to everyone why it is worth the effort, it must be fun in itself. How can we do positive things for others if we ourselves do not enjoy our own lives?

To make this concrete for a moment: an afternoon of collecting food from businesses that would have thrown it away and serving it to hungry people and people who are tired of working to pay for food—that is good political action, but only if you enjoy it. If you do it with your friends, if you meet new friends while you're doing it, if you fall in love or trade funny stories or just feel proud to have helped a woman by easing her financial needs, that's good political action. On the other hand, if you spend the afternoon typing an angry letter to an obscure leftist tabloid objecting to a columnist's use of the term "anarcho-syndicalist," that's not going to accomplish shit, and you know it.

Perhaps it is time for a new word for "politics," since you have made such a swear word out of the old one. For no one should be put off when we talk about acting together to improve our lives.

And so we present to you our demands, which are non-negotiable, and must be met *as soon as possible*—because we're not going to live forever, are we?

---

1. Make politics relevant to our everyday experience of life again. The farther away the object of our political concern, the less it will mean to us, the less real and pressing it will seem to us, and the more wearisome politics will be.

2. All political activity must be joyous and exciting in itself. You cannot escape from dreariness with more dreariness.

3. To accomplish those first two steps, entirely new political approaches and methods must be created. The old ones are outdated, outmoded. Perhaps they were NEVER any good, and that's why our world is the way it is now.

4. Enjoy yourselves! There is never any excuse for being bored... or boring!

Join us in making the "revolution" a *game*; a game played for the highest stakes of all, but a joyous, carefree game nonetheless!

THE CINEMA PRANK

rimethInc. operatives dressed in movie theater uniforms gave out 200 free passes to a showing of Natural Born Killers at a corporate chain movie theater in Chicago, Illinois. When a crowd, consisting of equal parts everything-for-free actionists and unsuspecting cinematophile coupon-clutchers, showed up expecting to be let into the showing for free, the managers first barred the doors and demanded to know who was responsible for the prank. But when it became clear that the crowd thought the theater managers were fucking with *them,* and began to get hostile, the managers realized the smartest thing they could do for their business would be to accept the coupons and let everyone in. Thus a core of impoverished CrimethInc. workers got to see a movie for free and radicalized a couple hundred civilians in the process. 🌸

☞ NOT WORKING CAN BE HARD WORK, PAGE 199

Honestly, when was the last time you spent a whole day just enjoying what you were doing and feeling? Enjoying it solely for its own sake, without thinking about the future or worrying about the long-term consequences?

When was the last time you spent a whole month living that way?

Do you have a hard time forgetting about your responsibilities, your goals, your productivity, and just being in the present?

Product is the *Excrement* of Action.

by Jeanette Winterson

Today, our lives revolve around *things*. We measure our worth in terms of our material possessions: in terms of our control over things outside ourselves. We gauge our success in life in terms of our "productivity"; that is, our ability to make these things. Our social system revolves around the production and consumption of material goods more than anything else. Even when we are not thinking about material objects, we represent our lives to ourselves as things: we consider our accomplishments, our future prospects, our social position . . . anything but how we actually *feel*. "The end justifies the means," we say; that is, the *products* of our actions, the end results of our lives, are more important to us than the process of living itself.

But products are the *excrement* of actions. Product is what is left over when the dust settles and the pulse returns to normal, when the day is done, when the coffin is laid in the ground. We do not exist in the settling dust or the scorecard; we are here in the present tense, in the making, the doing, the feeling. Just as we try to immortalize ourselves by fleeing into the world of fixed, deathless images, we try to externalize ourselves by thinking in terms of the results of our actions rather than our experience of the actions themselves. After all, it's so complicated to have to worry about whether you are really enjoying yourself, how you are feeling in the moment. It is easier to focus on the results, the hard evidence of your life; these things seem easier to understand, and easier to control.

Of course today's average worker is used to thinking about the ends rather than the means. He spends most of his time and energy working at a job that in all likelihood does not fulfill his dreams. He looks forward to payday every two weeks, for he counts on his paycheck to make sense out of his life: without it, he would feel like he was wasting his time. If he didn't look at the "consequences" of his actions as a justification for them, life would be unbearable—what if he constantly considered how he was feeling as he bagged groceries, or asked himself if he was having fun every moment he struggled with the fax machine? Insofar as his everyday experience of life is tedious and meaningless, he needs to concentrate on the coming weekend, the next vacation, his next purchases, to fend off insanity. And eventually he is bound to generalize that mode of thinking to other parts of his life: he comes to evaluate possible actions according to the rewards they offer, just as he would evaluate a job according to the wage it offers.

Thus, the present has lost almost all significance for modern man. Instead he spends his life always planning for the future: he studies for a diploma, rather than for the pleasure of learning; he chooses his job for social status, wealth, and "security," rather than for joy; he saves his money for big purchases and vacation trips, rather than to buy his way out of wage slavery and into full time freedom. When he finds himself experiencing profound happiness with another human being, he tries to freeze that moment, to turn it into a permanent fixture (a *contract*), by marrying her. On Sundays he goes to church, where he is told to do good deeds in order to one day receive eternal salvation

Modern society is centered around the production and distribution of material goods, rather than the happiness and satisfaction of its participants!

thus

Modern man thinks in terms of what he has " to show for it", rather than considering the life itself.

(as NietzsChe says, the good Christian still wants to be *paid well*), rather than for the sheer pleasure of helping others. The "aristocratic disregard for consequences," that ability to act for the sake of action that every hero possesses, is far beyond him.

It is a cliché that men and women of middle class and middle age have a hard time putting aside their insurance policies and investment programs to seize the moment; but, all too often, we, too, end up exchanging present for future and experience for souvenirs. We save mementos, trophies, boxes of keepsakes, old letters, as if life can be gathered, stored up, frozen for later . . . for later? For when? Life is here with us now, running through us like a river; and

like a river, it cannot be held in place without losing its magic. The more time we spend trying to "save it up," the less we have to throw ourselves into it.

The worst of us, in fact, are the radicals and artists. All too often, we "revolutionaries" expend our efforts thinking and talking about a revolution "that is to come," rather than concentrating on *making* revolution in the present tense. We're so used to thinking in terms of production that even when we try to make life into something immediate and exciting, we still end up centering our efforts around an event in the future. And like factory supervisors, we worry more about our productivity (the number of new believers recruited, the progress of the "cause," etc.) than about how we and our fellow human beings are feeling and living.

Artists suffer from this tendency most of all; for their vocation itself depends on making products out of the raw material of real-life experience. There is something of the capitalist's lust for domination in the way that artists mold their emotions and experiences into forms of their own making through the act of expression; for the expression of feelings and sensations, unique and unfathomable as they are, always consists of a kind of simplification. It isn't enough for the artist to just experience and appreciate life as it really is; she comes to cannibalize her life for what is really a *career,* a series of products outside herself, even adjusting her life for her career's sake. Worse, she may find that she cannot make love on a rooftop at daybreak without planning out the *excellent scene for her novel* (excrement!) this will make for.

Certainly, excretion is a healthy and necessary function of the soul as well as the body, and there is a place for art in our lives as a way to pour feeling back into the world when the heart is full to overflowing; but if you keep trying to do it after it is unnecessary, you eventually force out your heart and the rest of your insides (remember the fairy tale of the goose and the golden eggs?). We must put life and experience first, we must meet the world with only this in mind, as fresh and innocent as when we were children, with no intentions to cannibalize, categorize, organize, or simplify the profound infinities of our experiences. Otherwise, we will miss what is most vital, most beautiful, most immediate in this world, in our search for things that can be pressed flat and preserved "for all time." *Imagination should be used first and foremost to transform everyday reality, not just to make symbolic representations of it.* How many exciting novels could be written about the sort of lives that most of us lead these days, anyway? *Let us make living our art, rather than seeking to make mere art out of our lives.*

Let's stop "making history"—we're all so obsessed with "making a mark"—and start living. *That* would be a *real* revolution!

THE SECOND INTERNATIONAL

fter two years of the zero work experiment, it was clear to all the members of the CrimethInc. federation that it was time to share solutions to the inherent difficulties of the undertaking, and discuss what the next steps should be. A second CrimeIntern was convened at an abandoned fundamentalist church, with about one hundred women and men in attendance. The chief drawbacks of the no-work strategy, the delegates agreed, were that it was only viable for a select few, and that it tended to divest those who pursued it of access to some of the resources of the rest of society. It was decided that the next CrimethInc. project would have to be to re-integrate the ex-workers into wider circles of society, in order to work towards integrating more members of society into the circles of the ex-workers. Towards that end new CrimethInc. projects beyond stealing, dumpstering, and squatting were planned.

THE NEXT WACO CAN BE FOUND ON PAGE 204

**is for Sex
and Space**

Vanguard of the Sexual Revolution

An ad hoc committee consisting of all the people at any given time who are having sex that either is broadening to their personal horizons, is socially prohibited, or takes place in a barely concealed public space. It often includes fresh young lovers, reckless life-artist types, and men and women of all ages entering into unexpected affairs; masturbating adolescents who live with their parents are always considered honorary members. Conquest-seeking so-called "libertines" are excluded on principle, of course. Here is the V.S.R. manifesto, composed by Nadia C. in a library one night when she hadn't made love for an agitating three days . . . or perhaps on a still Christmas morning after a night of passionate sex with a woman she had wanted for years.

A call (in)to arms!

Because we get to have so little honest, intimate, beautifully *dangerous* sex that they can sell us flat images of it instead. Because we spend so much more time contemplating these *representations* than having sex that when we *do* sleep together, it is more a meeting of *roles* than of individuals—and not supportive or satisfying roles, at that. Because the most radical of us would still rather speak fancifully of total revolution than dare a moment of actual experimentation in a field that really matters, like our beds. Because as long as our own sexualities are constructed by the media of silence and the culture of violence, each of us is a Trojan horse bearing our own enemies (the fetishization of domination and submission, the paralysis of fear and shame) everywhere we go.

It's time to stop being spectators and start being actors (or agents, if you prefer, the double meaning being very much intended), to take our desires back by converting our sex lives from passive recreation into active re-creation. And to do this, we must first replace the representations of sex in our lives and all around us with *real sex*.

Our numbers are greater than you think. You are one of us each time you transform "public" space—*not* by "privatizing" it [it's already

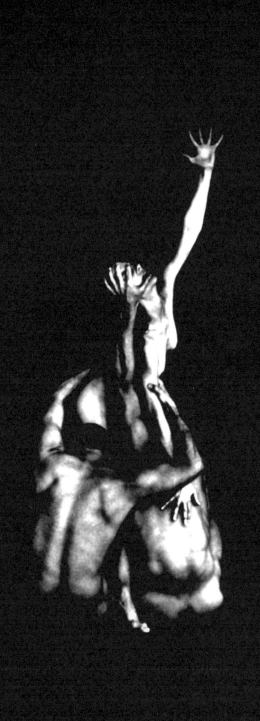

deprived of anything *personal* at all, thus the irony that the "public" is actually the least *public* of spaces], but by making it into real *people space,* by doing something in it that truly feels liberating . . . for example, fucking (on the roof of the police station, at the shore on the rocks just below the art museum window, etc.). Not that public sex is always itself revolutionary sex, but such sex is always revolutionary in that it takes lovemaking out of the narrow confines in which it is permitted—that is, in which it is permitted to *languish,* caged and stripped of the spontaneity that is its life's blood, just as we languish with the *rest* of the world stripped of *it.*

They shall know us by the innocence of our guilty smiles, holding hands as we walk out of the fog in parks at night: transformed and transcendent, unbowed and uninhibited in this dry and dreamless world—by used birth control devices(* and **) left in university classrooms and office bathrooms—by growing numbers of women who know exactly what they want and men who aren't afraid to touch one another. We will be the spark that ignites the new sexual revolution: armies of lovers laying down their responsibilities and picking up *each other,* as weapons, to fight against the smothering joylessness of this world. To quote the skinheads' anthem of homophobia and intolerance back at them, we refuse to "stay in the closet because it's safe in there"—precisely for that reason! As we've learned time and again in this struggle, *our only safety is in danger.*

Lovers of the world, unite—you have nothing to lose but your shame, and a world of pleasure to win!

Reprinted from the ninth annual Bulletin of Saboteurs. *For the revolution of the erotic and the erotica of revolution, contact: CrimethInc. Vice Squad*

* . . . although it's worth pointing out that most of the birth control methods/ devices in use in our culture today are themselves far from radical or liberating. Another aspect of the commodification of our lives in general and sexuality in particular is that we're supposed to buy a product for *everything,* even the most natural and personal of our activities, like sex . . . more often than not, a chemical product that fucks around with our bodies in a hundred scary ways, too. Look around and you'll see that there *are* alternatives . . . not just to the birth control methods on the market today, but also to the traditional ways of making love and being sexual that mainstream culture offers us.

**Of course there are those who will read this entire manifesto as an exhortation to littering, based on the extravagance of this single phrase . . . to such dreariness I can only respond with a merry FUCK YOU!

THE FIRST CRIMETHINC. COMPOUND OPENS

A CrimethInc. collective in Providence, Rhode Island opened the first CrimethInc. compound, known as Fort Thunder. The space is operated by a core of people who inhabit the building, working in cooperation with the surrounding community, for which the compound provides a shared place for all sorts of projects: a Food Not Bombs kitchen and cafe, a music and reading library, a free bicycle bank (operating in conjunction with other bicycle exchanges around the city, thus providing free and environmentally friendly individual transportation for the community), an artists' workshop, a public darkroom for photographers, a practice/performance space for bands, a stage for movie screenings, plays, and talent shows, a communal child care facility, even a sauna—all open to the public, of course, and organized with them at consensus meetings. Special events have included everything from underground film festivals to a mock Roman gladiator competition, complete with spinning cage and screaming crowd. In the years since, numerous similar compounds have been opened across the world (see illustration for sample floorplan). These spaces allow us CrimethInc. workers to survive with minimal "living expenses," and to link our welfare to that of others, rather than taking care of our own needs at everyone else's expense, as we're all expected to do.

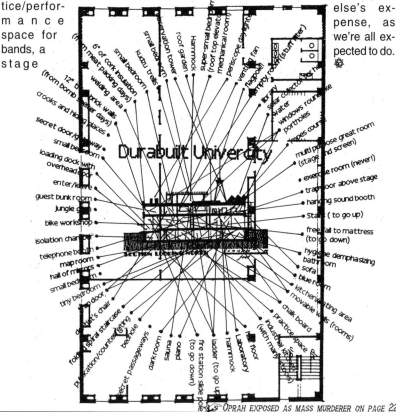

☞ OPRAH EXPOSED AS MASS MURDERER ON PAGE 220

AlieNation:
The Map of Despair

Space/Time Control, Space Travel, and Space Exploration

In the modern world, control is exerted over us automatically by the spaces we live and move in. We go through certain rituals in our lives—work, "leisure," consumption, submission—because our world is designed for these alone. We all know malls are for shopping, offices are for working, ironically-named "living" rooms are for watching television, and schools are for obeying teachers. All the spaces we travel in have pre-set meanings, and all it takes to keep us going through the same motions is to keep us moving along the same paths. It's hard to find anything to do in Walmart but look at and purchase merchandise; and, accustomed to this as we are, it's hard to conceive that there could be anything else we could do there anyway—not to mention that doing anything but shopping there is pretty much illegal, when you think about it.

There are fewer and fewer free, undeveloped spaces left in the world where we can let our bodies and minds run free. Almost every place you can go belongs to some person or group which has already designated a meaning and prescribed use for it: private estate, shopping district, superhighway, classroom, national park. And our very predictable routes through the world rarely take us near the free areas that do remain.

These spaces, where thought and pleasure can be free in every sense, are being replaced with carefully controlled environments like Disneyland—places in which our desires are prefabricated and sold back to us at our financial and emotional expense. Giving our own meaning to the world and creating our own ways to play and act in it are fundamental parts of human life; today, when we are never in spaces that encourage this, it should be no surprise that so many of us feel desperate and unfulfilled. But because the world has so little free space

atro*city*: The city is the organization of silence and isolation, humanity paralyzed as a perpetual motion machine.

Tourism: The process by which a space that has not been allocated for production or housing (i.e. the eradication of real life) is turned into a place where fake life can be had—for a price.

l e f t
in it, and
the circuitry of
our everyday lives
never takes us there,
we're forced to go to
places like Disneyland for
any semblance of play
and excitement at all.
The real adventure our

hearts crave has been largely replaced by fake adventure, and the thrill of creation by the drill of spectatorship.

Our time is as thoroughly occupied and regulated as our space; indeed, the subdivision of our space is a manifestation of what has already happened to our time. The entire world moves and lives according to a standardized time system, designed to synchronize our movements from one side of the planet to the other.

the distance between individuals **within** those communities widens.

A curious effect of the development of rapid transit systems is that as the distance between communities closes,

Inside of this larger system, we all have our lives regimented by our work schedules and/or school hours, as well as the hours that public transportation runs and businesses operate, etc. This scheduling of our lives, which begins in childhood, exerts a subtle but deep control over us all: we come to forget that the time of our lives is ultimately *ours* to spend how we choose, and instead think in terms of work days, lunch hours, and weekends. A truly spontaneous life is unthinkable to most of us; and so-called "free" time is usually just time that has been scheduled for something other than work. How often do you get to see the sun rise? How many sunny afternoon walks do you get to take? If you had the unexpected opportunity to take an exciting trip this week, could you do it?

These restricting environments and schedules drastically limit the vast potential of our lives. They also keep us isolated from each other. At our jobs, we spend a great deal of time doing one particular kind of labor with one particular group of people, in one set place (or at least in one set environment, for construction workers and "temp" employees). Such limited, repetitive experience gives us a very limited perspective on the world, and keeps us from coming to know people from other backgrounds. Our homes isolate us further: today we keep ourselves locked apart in little boxes, partly out of fear of those capitalism has treated even worse than ourselves, and partly because we believe the paranoia propaganda of the companies that sell security systems. Today's suburbs are cemeteries of community, the people packed

Space does not *exist* until it is explored. One *creates* space by running, leaping, dancing, climbing through it.

separately into boxes . . . just like our supermarket products, sealed for "freshness." With thick walls between us and our neighbors, and our friends and families scattered across cities and nations, it's hard to have any kind of community at all, let alone share community space in which people can benefit from each other's creativity. And both our homes and our jobs keep us tied down to one place, stationary, unable to travel far through the world except on hasty vacations.

Even our travel is restricted and restricting. Our modern methods of transportation—cars, buses, subways, trains, airplanes—all keep us locked onto fixed tracks, watching the outside world go by through a screen, as if it were a particularly boring television show. Each of us lives in a personal world that consists mostly of well-known destinations (the workplace, the grocery store, a friend's apartment, the dance club) with a few links in between them (sitting in the car, standing in the subway, walking up the staircase), and little chance to encounter anything unexpected or discover any new places. A man could travel the freeways of ten nations without seeing anything but asphalt and gas stations, so long as he stayed in his car. Locked onto our tracks, we can't imagine truly *free* travel, voyages of discovery that would bring us into direct contact with brand new people and things at every turn.

Instead, we sit in traffic jams, surrounded by hundreds of people in the same predicament as ourselves, but separated from them by the steel cages of our cars—so they appear to us as objects in our way rather than fellow human beings. We think we are reaching more of the world with our modern transportation; but in fact we see less of it, if anything. As our transportation capabilities increase, our cities sprawl farther and farther across the landscape. Whenever travel distances increase, more cars are needed; more cars demand more space, and thus distances increase again . . . and again. At this rate highways and gas stations will one day replace everything that was worth traveling to in the first place . . . everything that hasn't already been turned into a theme park or a tourist attraction, that is.

Some of us look at the internet as the "final frontier," as a free, undeveloped space still ripe for exploring. Cyberspace may or may not offer some degree of freedom to those who can afford to use and explore it; but whatever it might offer, it offers on the condition that we check our bodies at the door: voluntary amputation. Remember, you are a body at least as much as a mind: is it freedom to sit, stationary, staring at glowing lights for hours, without using your senses of taste, touch, or smell? Have you forgotten the sensations of wet grass

or warm sand under bare feet, of eucalyptus tree or hickory smoke in your nostrils? Do you remember the scent of tomato stems? The glint of candlelight, the thrill of running, swimming, touching?

Today we can turn to the internet for excitement without feeling like we have been cheated because our modern lives are so constrained and predictable that we have forgotten how joyous action and motion in the real world can be. Why settle for the very limited freedom that cyberspace can provide, when there is so much more experience and sensation to be had out here in the real world? We should be running, dancing, canoeing, drinking life to the dregs, exploring new worlds— *what* new worlds? We must rediscover our bodies, our senses, the space around us, and then we can transform this space into a new world to which we can impart meanings of our own.

To this end, we need to invent new games—games that can take place in the conquered spaces of this world, in the shopping malls and restaurants and classrooms, that will break down their prescribed meanings so that we can give them new meanings in our accordance with our own dreams and desires. We need games that will bring us together, out of the confinement and isolation of our private homes, and into public spaces where we can benefit from each other's company and creativity. Just as natural disasters and power outages can bring people together and be exciting for them (after all, they do make for a little thrilling variety in an otherwise drearily predictable world), our games will join us together in doing new and exciting things. We

If your heart is free, the ground you're standing on is liberated territory. Defend it.

should have poetry painted on the walls of the shopping districts, concerts in the streets, sex in the parks and classrooms, free picnics in supermarkets, spontaneous festivals on freeways . . .

We need to invent new conceptions of time and new modes of travel, as well. Try living without a clock, without synchronizing your life with the rest of the busy, busy world. Try taking a long trip on foot or bicycle, so that you will encounter everything that you pass between your starting point and your destination firsthand, without a screen. Try exploring in your own neighborhood, looking on rooftops and around corners you never noticed before—you'll be amazed how much adventure is hidden there waiting for you!

Our present maps describe a world no human being has ever set foot in: a world of carefully measured distances and standardized symbols, frozen in time, empty of emotional ambiances—an *objective* world, when today we all know that there is no world but the *subjective*. These maps hold so little information of real relevance to human life that it is no wonder we get so lost using them: around and around in circles we go, arriving "on time" at our supposed destinations, with no real idea of where we're bound or why, let alone what there is to be found in this world beyond interstate highways and Newark, New Jersey.

If we made our maps ourselves, plotting our individual experiences rather than the data provided by our instruments, they would reveal clearly what it is like to be a human being in this world. Perhaps then we could go about creating a world for *human beings* to live in, not instruments. A book like *On the Road* is an example of one of these maps: it charts the paths of a few individuals through space and time, chronicling the traffic of their hearts as well as the motion of their bodies. Granted, it might not be much use for figuring out street di-

REAL MAPS OF THE IMAGINARY WORLD, IMAGINARY MAPS OF THE REAL WORLD.

rections to a gas station in Denver, but in the long run it will help you get a lot farther than a road map of Colorado ever could.

It's true that we all experience the world differently, and that if we make our maps sincerely (i.e. subjectively) they will all look different; but that should be cause to celebrate the breadth of the world, not to grumble! And just as a novel about people you have never met can serve as a useful map for your own life, these very individual records can often be useful for many other people, and in a variety of ways. You'll find that if you speak honestly for yourself, you are probably speaking for others as well: that's a part of being human (and our excuse for throwing around the word "we" so mercilessly in these pages). Here follow some subjective maps that participants in our collective have made, as examples; this book itself is a map too, of course, if you use it right.

8. I wondered what I'd left behind.

11. Your letters pressed against my wet cheek

1. We were young and strange and we transformed space.

10. And my hands were filled with shifting sand.

Loversong

by Gloria Cubana

Here your eyes reflected yellow flowers 9.

16. And the world seemed bigger than it ever had before.

3. promised to bring you here and make you fall in love.

And your hands on me here in that starry field. 2.

The night's pulse made me dizzy 13.

And I sobbed on a foreign street for the loss of you. 14.

What savage desire moved within me?

The delirium and fright of freedom.

7. And I spoke to your absence in the warm dark.

15. The orange sun slipped slowly behind dark hills

8. We felt a wild strength here inside us

6. I found my own voice

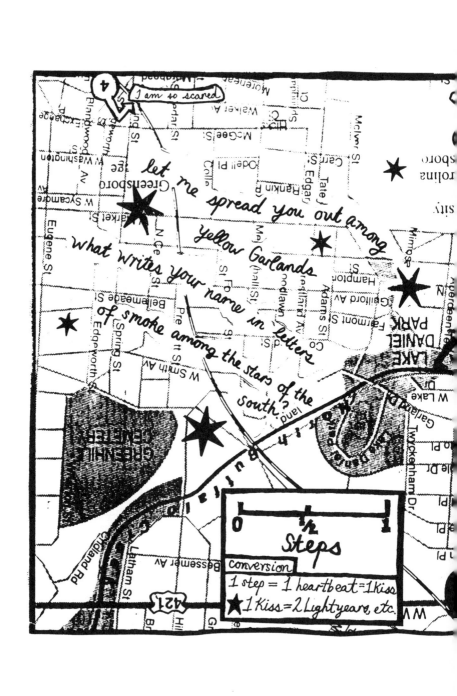

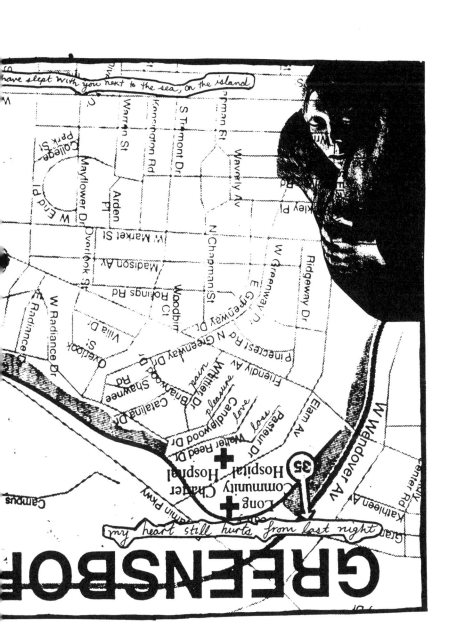

① individual resonance chamber.
② system instrument as four independent partial mass
③ function of displacement, a system of two kinematic

g risks....

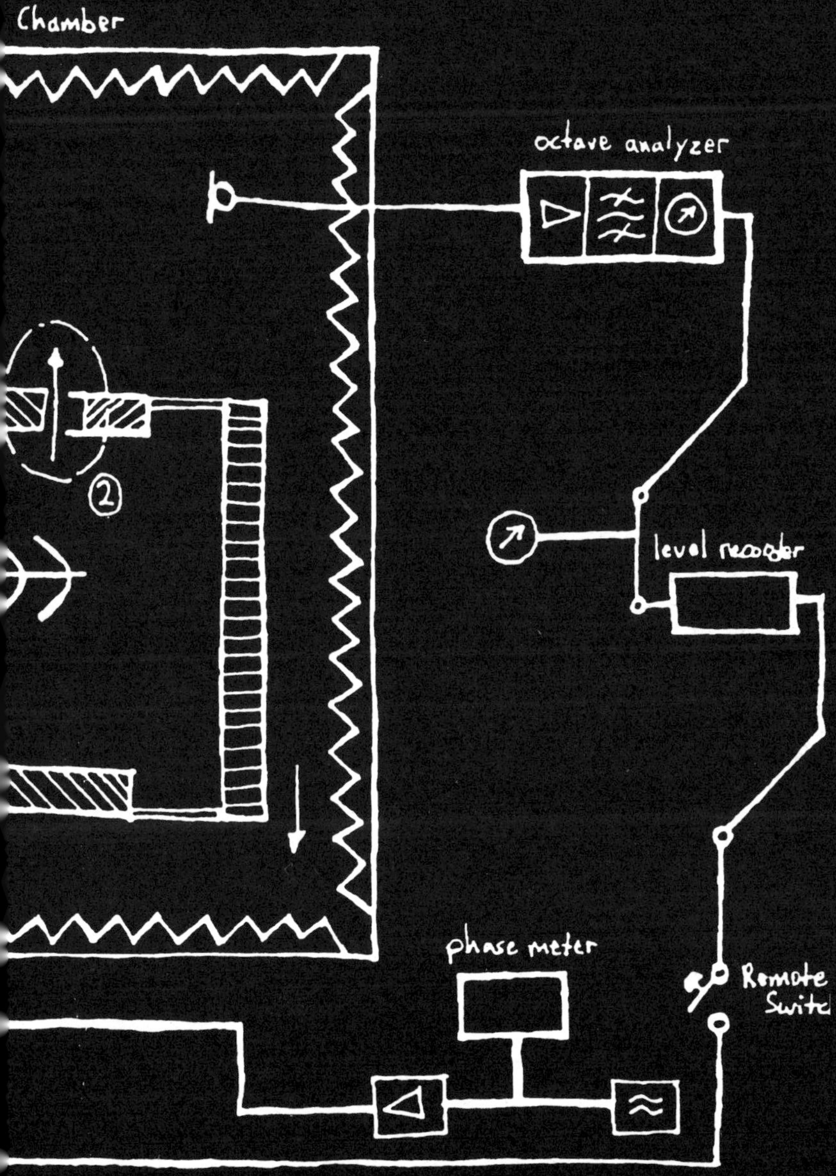

Chamber

octave analyzer

②

level recorder

phase meter

Remote
Switc

us communication.
of freedom.

my house. Each time, I took a new route, but I always pa

Legend: 1. I walked (————) a series of journeys (♡) in the woods surounding

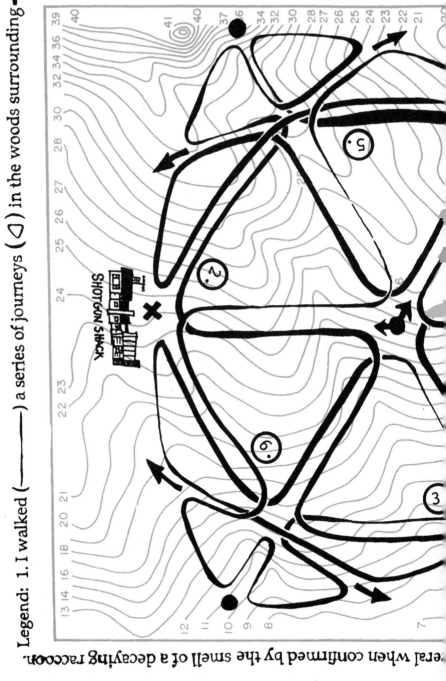

SHOTGUN SHACK

...eral when confirmed by the smell of a decaying raccoon.

place where a raccoon () had died. 2. With each visit, its carcass testified to the passage of time. 3. My orientation shifted from where to when, not the theoretical when of a calendar b

SURFACE I
SPATIAL, TOPOGRAPHIC, LINEAR

SURFACE II
TEMPORAL, PSYCHOGRAPHIC, CYCLICAL

SHOTGUN SHACK

SHOTGUN SHACK

THE HIJACKING OF THE WASHINGTON POST

In response to the constant stream of misinformation from the mainstream media about the case of the so-called "Unabomer," a CrimethInc. commando team led by a low-ranking graphic designer in the advertising department of the Washington Post removed an advertisement for pantyhose from the first section of the Sunday Edition and replaced it with this hot-headed tirade:

The Unabomber: A Hero For Our Time

"I've killed more people than the Unabomber because I've paid more taxes than he has." –Oprah Winfrey

Pop quiz: what is it called when one of the finest minds of a generation picks a few individuals who are personally involved in the destruction of the environment (a timber-industry lobbyist) or of the attention span and reasoning ability of tens of thousands of Americans (an advertising executive), and kills or maims them in the pursuit of finding a voice for his concerns about social issues . . . concerns that otherwise would be heard by very few?

Clearly, it is murder.

And what is it called when a nation of overweight barbers and underpaid clerks, of lazy unemployed middle class intellectuals and talk-show-educated housewives, of cowardly fast-food-chain managers and racist sorority girls, conspires to execute this murderer in the name of protecting the glorious status quo from his obviously deranged "mad bombings"?

The death penalty. And rightly applied, too, in defense of the right of forest clear-cutters and professional liars

to continue bending our world to their vision without the danger of being molested by those who prefer redwood forests to Quik-Marts and folk songs to detergent slogans.

Seriously, and rhetoric aside, what is the difference between the two situations? In one case, a single person evaluates his situation and decides upon a course of action he feels is right. In the other case, millions of people, who are not very used to making up their minds by themselves, feel strong enough all together to strike out blindly against an individual who does not remain within their boundaries of acceptable behavior.

Now, our gentle and moderate reader would no doubt like to object that it is not fear of the free-standing individual that prompts the outcry against this terrorist, but moral indignation—for he has taken "innocent" life in his quest to have his ideas heard, and that is wrong in every situation.

But this nation of petty imbeciles is not regularly outraged about the taking of innocent life: as long as it fits within the parameters of the status quo, they don't care at all.

How many more people than the Unabomber have tobacco companies maimed and killed, by using advertising to addict them at a very young and uninformed age to an extremely harmful drug? How about the companies that advertise and sell cheap liquor in impoverished neighborhoods filled with alcoholics? How many citizens of third world nations have suffered and died at the hands of governments supported by such corporations as Shell Oil, or even by the U.S. government itself? And how much animal life is destroyed thoughtlessly every year, every day in

America
is voting for the
UNABOMBER

death camp factory farms . . . or in ecological destruction brought about by such companies as Exxon (our reader will remember the Valdez) or McDonalds (one of the better known destroyers of the rainforest)? No one is particularly concerned about these abuses of "innocent" life.

And indeed, it is harder to be, for they are institutionalized within the social and economic system . . . "normal." Besides, it is hard to figure out who exactly is responsible for them, for they are the results of the workings of complicated bureaucracies inside an even more complicated social/economic system.

On the other hand, when one individual attempts to make his criticism of this destructive system heard by one of the only really effective means, it is easy to pick him out and string him up. And our hypocritical outrage about his wrongdoings compared those of our own social institutions shows that it is his ability to act upon his own conclusions that truly shocks and frightens us most of all.

Our fear of the Unabomber as a freely acting individual shows in the attempts our media has made to demonize him. Aspects of his character, such as his academic prowess and his ability to live a Thoreauan self-sufficient existence, which would normally occasion praise, are now used to demonstrate that he is a maladjusted freak. Random and unimportant details of his life, similar to details of any of our lives, such as failed love affairs and childhood illnesses, are used to explain his "insane behavior." In speaking thus, representatives of the press suggest that there is no question at all that his actions were the result of insanity, pulling away in terror from the very thought that he might be just as rational as they . . . or more so. Newspapers print the most arbitrary and disconnected excerpts of his manifesto that they can combine, then describe the manifesto as being random and disconnected— they even describe it as "ramblings" with a straight face, despite the well-known short attention span of today's media.

But it is not necessary that we accept the media's typical over-simplification of the case. The Unabomber's manifesto has, as a result of his efforts, been published and widely distributed. We can all read it for ourselves, not just in disconnected excerpts, but in its entirety, and decide for ourselves what we think of his ideas.

Do not be frightened by the Unabomber's willingness to stand out from the crowds and take whatever actions he believes are necessary to achieve his goals. In a civilization so stricken with mindless submission to social norms and irrational rules his example should be refreshing rather than horrifying; for his worst crimes are no worse than ours, in being citizens of this nation . . . and his greatest deeds as a dedicated and intelligent individual far outshine those of most of our heroes, who are for the most part basketball players and cookie-cutter pop musicians anyway.

At least, given the chance as we are, we should read his manifesto and come to our own conclusions, rather than allowing the press and popular opinion/paranoia to decide for us. ✿

☞ ART-TERRORISM AT ITS FINEST ON PAGE 234

**is for Technology
and Theft**

(from Jeanette Winterson's response to a letter from her friend William Gibson:)

WHEN WE

Today, technological innovation itself commands too much of our attention and energy. We use a disproportionate amount of our collective creativity inventing new technologies to dominate the world, rather than discovering new ways to enjoy it. This reflects an underlying theme in our civilization: our values tend to revolve around control rather than pleasure. We have put all our capabilities into adjusting the "how" of life, without stopping to address the "why."

Some claim that recklessly rapid technological development is inherent to any industrial society. It seems equally likely that it is a result of the pressure the capitalist economy exerts on businesses and inventors to keep coming up with new products to outmode the old ones. A truly non-capitalist society, in which competition for sales and survival did not exist, might be able to make the best of the technologies it had at its disposal rather than continually trying to develop more complexity for its own sake. Technology itself would be deployed differently in those conditions, as well (e.g. more public transportation, fewer cars and highways and pollution), making it less of a threat to human happiness and freedom.

But there are still important questions to consider. First of all, how much of today's technology would be possible at all in a non-capitalist, non-hierarchical society? Today power is centralized in the hands of technocrats who direct unbelievably complex global networks. It is these systems that produce the unbelievably complex technologies we are accustomed to. Is radically direct

The television will not be revolutionized.

democracy and group decision-making even possible on such a huge scale? Probably not. The question, then, is how much of our technological complexity we could take with us in the process of decentralizing our society.

And it still remains to consider the pros and cons of individual technologies. Under radically different circumstances, could automobiles, e-mail, television, neon lights be used to make our lives more exciting and rewarding? For some of them, the answer is probably yes, while for others, no. When evaluating the worth of particular technologies, we must always remember that our activities and environment are shaped as much by the tools we use as they are shaped by our applications of the tools themselves. For example, using the internet for communication involves sitting stationary for minutes or hours, staring at a glowing screen, isolated from the world of the senses, surrounded by and yet separated from others, as one is in a traffic jam (thus people communicating anonymously through the internet often show each other the same courtesy they would in rush hour traffic); it also replaces forms of communication that are less mediated. In a paradise, would this be a part of everyday life?

When action seems impossible "Communication" is consolation.

USE TOOLS

You talk about using the tools of the system to destroy the system—but if some of these tools create alienation by their very use, they can only adjust and ultimately reinforce the system of alienation. Rather than taking for granted the official line that "more technology is better," and accepting the linear conception of history taught to us by the ideology of "progress" (i.e. humanity goes from a less technological to a more technological state, never the other way around), we should be willing to make whatever alterations are necessary in the technology used by our species in order to get the most out of life that we can.

And yes, we should use whatever tools will work in this struggle, but only the ones that really will work. Let's be wary of every technology, and dare to believe that we really can leave behind the ones that are no use to us.

To make these generalizations concrete, I'm frankly very frightened by the antiquated image of a technologically engineered utopia that you conjure up with your computer-guided cars. I can barely repair a car myself at this point; do you realize that if everything were guided by computers, the ability to fix and control everything would be left in the hands of a tiny minority, the ones who had the special proficiencies required? The average person would feel very little understanding of or control over the world she lived in. All the practical aspects of life would be left up to the "experts." We're almost there, already, and it makes the world an alien and confusing place for most of us, doesn't it? Is "progress" really so inexorable that I shouldn't dare ask for this to be different?

With all our new capabilities for communication and mobility, we're paralyzed running in place. In a world where information equals power, the most powerful are the ones who are willing to be immobilized in every real sense in order to function better as information processors. Unplug yourself from the circuitry! Mobilize!

(. . . and Stella Nera's critique of Jeanette's response:)

THEY USE

Oh Cyberspace, what big eyes and ears you have!

It was once said that the map is not the terrain. The speaker meant to point to the limits of human abstraction in friction with full reality. But we are now being herded with electronic prods from the terrain to the map, from the real to the virtual—soon there will be no friction! Simulated electronic space is a map, merely a map: the better to simplify, rationalize, describe, monitor, predict, propagandize, con-

Progress—

Forward, into what?

tain, and control you with. Cyberspace is a closed playpen, where everything is permitted, but nothing is possible. Use cyberspace to get information? When you use cyberspace, you get *in formation*.

Interactive communication has become a form of invisible control. Cyberspace integrates us into a neural network; together, we become the extended brain of the technological system. The more interconnected the population, the faster propaganda diffuses. Yesterday's control by communication: politicians polled the public, processed the results, and

***A new design for relationships,
Relationships of distance.
Relationships which don't require meeting,
Relationships which require never meeting.***

adjusted their rhetoric to correct image problems. Today's control by communication: the outfitting of employees with pagers, cell phones, email accounts, voice mail . . . it is interesting to note how the current theme of propaganda is that consumers need more information—and therefore must not only plug themselves into the system, but must also carry an array of communication devices with them wherever they go.

And the future? The days of watching the Spectacle are almost over. The audience storms the stage: now *we* are the Spectacle, and propaganda is obsolete.

In the future, we will no longer be misled and distracted from reality by the media and other forces. We ourselves will become the distractions, interacting with each other in a medium in which no reality is possible. We remove ourselves from reality into Cyberspace.

US BACK.

We're now at full speed

And no one's at the wheel

Nostalgia for an unpredictable future

In this system, we work for the sake of organization. And organization increases, which increases work. The harder and faster we work, the more work there will be to do. Humans—originally carefree and free-ranging—have been tied down, first to the farm, then to the city factory, then to the office, and now to the computer monitor's virtual glo-grid. Thirty years ago offices didn't have PCs or cubes. How many of us today are forced to sit solitary under fluorescent bulbs in windowless gray cubes most of our waking hours (most of our *lives*) in front of a computer monitor, staring at flickering blue nothing, listening to high-pitched machine hum, making tiny movements with our fingers to manipulate symbols that have no vital meaning to us, all the while subconsciously panicked by pervasive surveillance? Forget the whole dynamic complex of simultaneous coercion, persuasion, socialization, sticks, carrots and credit that condemn us to the console. Would we do this if instead we could just live our lives, foraging in one way or another, eating, socializing, fucking, fantasizing, sleeping, drawing, singing, dancing, just being human, unemployed, not in use, free, free of fabricated goals? Subsistence would be such a luxury, compared to the "luxuries" we have.

Human minds are transformed into information-processors. (At least with physical labor your mind is free to fantasize.) We are degraded into serving machines—processing raw reality into computer logic data (scanning products at a cash register, data entry). We are used more and more as either physical robots or translators, that is, as interfaces between computerized systems. In the service industry, the food chain gang must wear

WE MAY PITY THEIR IGNORANCE AND POVERTY, BUT *THEY* PROBABLY FELT THAT NATURE WAS BOUNTIFUL, FOOD RIDICULOUSLY EASY TO GET, AND POSSESSIONS A USELESS BURDEN IN A NOMADIC LIFE!

CRAZY!

uniforms and logos, recite scripts, weigh scoops of ice cream while wearing plastic gloves. *Machines cast us in their images.*

Technology uses people, people do not use technology. Technology is not any single isolated object, it is a unified system of relationships between elements and systems. Those who claim that technology is a "neutral tool" or that it is an accumulation of independent "things" to be picked through selectively for keepers, fail to realize that technology is a metaphysical whole, that it is an expression of organization, and therefore can only direct itself toward higher order, increased centralized control, and the inevitable degradation of its human components. The metabolic flow must speed faster in pursuit of total productivity. We can always be more efficient, but we can never be efficient enough.

The electronic fist comes in molded beige plastic, beeping. Suddenly we all do Windows, and he who will not compute will not eat. And as our work, so our play: both are communication. To be silent or un-in-formed is to be anti-social. Evermore we will be engulfed in the electronic, starved of light, fresh air, fresh food, spontaneous movement, friendly face-to-face human company, human warmth, human smell, human touch, animals no more. We struggle: depression, agoraphobia, addiction, bulimia, panic, obsession-compulsion, suicides. And doctors medicate.

Our pre-pacification ancestor the cavewoman would never have sat still for this. Nor our four year old selves. But cyberspace disperses the crowd, and clears the streets. We are living in the post-riot era, inside our cubicles (office blocks, suburban blocks, cell blocks), staring at the screens, being entertained.

IF MODERN HUNTER-GATHERER SOCIETIES ARE ANY INDICATION, THE AVERAGE *HOMO ERECTUS* SPENT ONLY *4-5 HOURS* A DAY AT "WORK" AND THE REST IN RITUAL OR CREATIVE LOAFING.'

LOOK! I INVENT!

Here Is Folk Science!

Yes, the problem has been solved
But *I* never saw it proved.
Someone else has, but I have not,
Landed on the moon.
   -*Sera White, "A Momentary Gain of My Loss; or, Fragments"*

There is nothing wrong with tools, technology, and science. As a species, we are nothing if not the inventors and builders of our world; but as individuals, we have the capacity to determine what world we want, and to build it ourselves. When we do this, we seize the adventure, the invention . . . the inventure! that is our birthright. This is folk science.

Folk science is not new, it is as old as humanity—lab coats, the scientific method, and centralized top-down technology are new. As we progress, we will learn to view these things as aberrations of the innate scientific creativity that is a part of each person. As folk scientists, we will see that consensus science, with its universal explanations and solutions, taught us to distrust our own ingenuity, creativity, and intuition.

Folk Science Vs. "The" Scientific Method

The scientific method is a universal format and language for experimentation. Among other things, the scientific method is a way of packaging the results of one scientist's inquiry so that they are accessible to other scientists. Thus the scientific method acts as a net combining the efforts of all of the world's scientists. Using this powerful Babylonian tool, scientists cooperate to surpass our every need and bring us into their modernity ever faster and more efficiently.

As a scientific-method-driven phenomenon, modernity tells us that there is no use for repeating. This view is the source of the oft-heard comment "that's been done," a retort tantamount to death for a scientific act. Used in this way, the scientific method becomes a method for encouraging the progress of the group over the progress of the individual.

"Still powerful lords of universe, sooner or later you will give us machines to play with, or we will be forced to build them ourselves—to occupy the free time which you, with insane eagerness, wish to see us squander on trivialities and brain death."

–Henry "Adolph" Ford's rebellious daughter Marianne,
in a letter from her rural commune.

So our critique of "The Scientific Method" skips "Science" because it is a fundamental tool of our species, skips "Method," for method is the enactment of science but finds "The" guilty of a crime. This tyranny of "The" is part of a language that attempts to unify the menagerie of human curiosity and struggle into just one investigative technique and in doing so fails both science and humanity.

Folk Science and Art

At the root, art and science are the same. Both of these pursuits use the observation and experience that are part of every life as a basis for creative thought, ingenuity and producktion. But as science has become universalized and gathered up into the hands of the few, it has come to alienate the many.

The alienation of consensus science has also infected art. From Colour Field Painting to canned shit, art has become a that's-been-done style endgame. This process is encouraged when critics and historians who love logic, order, and their jobs support art that contributes to the linear progress of art history. This is art in a technological mode.

In the face of a system that cares only for final products, folk scientists reclaim the processes of scientific and artistic *discovery* as inherently valuable. Folk scientists see the beauty, adventure and relevance of reinventing the wheel*. So a phrase like "that's been done" is dribble to the folk scientist, who will respond: "not by me." By holding invention as a form of play, folk scientists are free from the tradition of linear progress that has stolen creativity from the uninitiated and made science and art into unattainable priesthoods.

The Folk Science of Love

Professional scientists have become intermediaries between us and our world; but nowadays these intermediaries can be found everywhere. These doctors, designers, evangelists and psychologists are a priest caste in the business of connecting the lowly individual to the universe, health, god, happiness, even love.

I want to think that, had I not seen kissing on television, I would have spontaneously come up with this bizarre interaction, but I can't know. We are so saturated with icons of love in mass media that, like science and art, this natural impulse becomes the business of experts. These sleek actors and porn stars let us fumble with our awkward bodies, botched lines and improper lighting, then step up show us how it's really done. The greatest achievement of any lovers is to transcend the bombardment of glossy images and find their own way.

So Here Is Folk Science...

... where we make it a daily practice to find our own way. Here, it's not too late to invent the airplane, the bicycle, the kiss. Here, there is room for inquiry into gravity, cancer, psychology, and anthills. Here, incredulous, we set out to see if the world is round—and find that it is not.

So don't spend your money, which wears away like the soles of your shoes. Spend your ingenuity, which is alive and becomes sharper with wear—spend your time, which, combined with ingenuity, seems ever more abundant—spend your life, the only gift you can hoard jealously and give graciously at the same time.

Deploy!

brief explanation of bike

Safety Bike: *Product of a two week Thinktank.*
Equipped with dual front brakes.
Instructions: *Go fast, brake hard, flip forward rolling on steel*
roll cage, land on two wheels, ride off victorious.

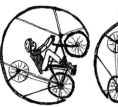

*Reinventing the Wheel: Agent F. Markatos Dixon is shown here indicating the gyroscopic stabilizer of his "Safety Bike." Dixon comments that while making the Safety Bike was easily as much fun for him as making an airplane was for the Wright brothers, the safety bike is unlikely to kill millions in crashes, be used to bomb civilians, or contribute to the death of the planet. "True!" quips Kit Carson, his hopping mad assistant, "and no one can disprove the Safety Bike!"

CRIMETHINC. FINISHES THE JOB FOR DADA

F. Markatos Dixon, member of the Paul F. Maul Artists' Group, entered his latest project, the Sub-Sub-Contra-Bass-Blaster, in a prestigious Manhattan art exhibition. The Sub-Sub-Contra-Bass-Blaster is an enormous apparatus that functions as a kind of homemade speaker, which emits the lowest frequencies of sound audible to humans. At opening night, when celebrities and critics from all over New York had gathered to sip champagne and swap literary references at the gallery, the proprietor asked Dixon to demonstrate his creation. When it was switched on, the deep tones of the 'Blaster ripped it loose from its poorly constructed base, and sent it leaping and starting around the gallery, paparazzi and starlets fleeing in terror before it. It smashed from wall to wall, decimating most of the sculptures and paintings in the room (for an estimated total damage of some $240,000), and was able to chase almost the entire public in attendance (with the exception of Dixon, who stood aside, laughing hysterically) into the street, thanks to a built-in power generator, before finally shaking itself into pieces which lay vibrating on the sidewalk before a crowd of horrified onlookers. Dixon grabbed the tray of cookies off the buffet table and disappeared out the back door, turning up later only to 'dissuade' the gallery owners from pressing charges—and inquire about his commission. ☾

---

spring 1998
CRIMETHINC. BALLET TROUPES DEBUT

A small army of people dressed in unwieldy costumes with restricted vision were directed by choreographer Jane E. Humble as they blundered through an unannounced performance of Marcel Duchamp's Rite of Spring for the benefit of specialists attending the yearly conference held by the *Journal of Atomic Scientists*. ✿

POLICE: THE GLUE THAT HOLDS US APART, PAGE 242

"In a world turned upside down, you have to be a thief to be an honest man."
—Mike Fromage, author of *Gehenna: One Man's Quest for Vengeance*

Why I Love Shoplifting

from big corporations
by. um. anonymous

featuring our friends, the mischievous Soy Milk and Tofu

Nothing compares to the feeling of elation, of burdens being lifted and constraints escaped, that I feel when I walk out of a corporate store with their products in my pockets. In a world where everything already belongs to someone else, where I am expected to sell away my life at work in order to get the money to pay for the minimum I need to sur-

vive, where I am surrounded by forces beyond my control or comprehension that obviously are not concerned about my needs or welfare, it is a way to carve out a little piece of the world for myself—to act back upon a world that acts so much upon me.

It is an entirely different sensation than the one I feel when I buy something. When I pay for something, I'm making a trade; I'm offering the money that I bought with my labor, my time, and my creativity for a product or service that the corporation wouldn't share with me under any other circumstances. In a sense, we have a relationship based on violence: we negotiate an exchange not according to our respect or concern for each other, but according to the forces that we can bring to bear on each other. Supermarkets know they can charge me a dollar for bread because I will starve if I do not buy it; they know they can't charge me four dollars, because I will buy it somewhere else. So our interaction revolves around unspoken threats, rather than love, and I am forced to give up something of my own to get anything from them[9].

Everything changes when I shoplift. I'm no longer negotiating with faceless, inhuman entities that have no concern for my welfare; instead, I'm taking what I need without giving anything up. I no longer feel like I am being forced into an exchange, and I no longer feel as if I have no control over the way the world around me dictates my life. I no longer have to worry about whether the pleasure I receive from the book I purchased was equal to the two hours of labor it cost me to be able to afford it. In these and a thousand other ways, shoplifting

---

[9] In a love relationship, conversely, people usually think of themselves as benefiting from giving to others, and vice versa.

makes me feel liberated and empowered. Let's examine what shoplifting has to offer as an alternative way of consuming.

The shoplifter wins her prize by taking risks, not by exchanging a piece of her life for it. Life for her is not something that must be sold away for seven or eight dollars an hour in return for survival; it is something that is hers because she takes it for herself, because she lays claim to it. In stark contrast to the law-abiding consumer, the means by which she acquires goods is as exciting as the goods themselves; and this means is also, in many ways, more praiseworthy.

Shoplifting is a refusal of the exchange economy. It is a denial that people deserve to eat, live, and die based on how effectively they are able to exchange their labor and capital with others. It is a denial that a monetary value can be ascribed to everything, that having a piece of delicious chocolate in your mouth is worth exactly fifty cents or that an hour of one person's life can really be worth ten dollars more than that of another person. It is a refusal to accept the capitalist system, in which workers have to buy back the products of their own labor at a profit to the owners of capital, who get them coming and going.

But what if they won't give it to me?

Take it!

Shoplifting says *NO* to all the objectionable features that have come to characterize the modern corporation. It is an expression of discontent with the low wages and lack of benefits that so many exploiting corporations force their employees to suffer in the name of company profits. It is a refusal to pay for low quality products that have been designed to break or wear out soon in order to force consumers to buy more. It is a refusal to fund the environmental damage that so many corporations perpetrate heartlessly in the course of manufacturing their products and building new stores, a refusal to support the corporations that run private, local businesses into bankruptcy, a refusal to accept the

murder of animals in the meat and dairy industries and the exploitation of migrant labor in the fruit and vegetable industries. Shoplifting makes a statement against the alienation of the modern consumer. "If we are not able to find or afford any products other than these, that were made a thousand miles from us and about which we can know nothing," it asserts, "then we refuse to pay for these."

The shoplifter attacks the cynical mind control tactics of modern advertising. Today's commercials, billboards, even the floor-layouts and product displays in stores are designed by psychologists to manipulate potential consumers into purchasing products. Corporations carry out extensive advertising campaigns to insinuate their exhortations to consumption into every mind, and even work to make their products into status symbols that people from some walks of society eventually *must* own in order to be accorded respect. Faced with this kind of manipulation, the law-abiding consumer has two choices: either to come up with the money to purchase these products by selling his life away as a wage laborer, or to go without and possibly invite public ridicule as well as private frustration. The shoplifter creates a third choice of her own: she takes the products she has been conditioned to desire without paying for them, so the corporations themselves must pay for all of their propagandizing and mind control tactics.

Shoplifting is the most effective protest against all these objectionable attributes of modern corporations because it is not merely theoretical—it is practical, it involves action. Verbal protests can be raised to irresponsible business practices without ever having any solid effect, but shoplifting is intrinsically damaging these corporations at the same time as it (however covertly) demonstrates dissatisfaction. It is better than a boycott, because not only does it *cost* the corporation money rather than just denying it profit, it also means that the shoplifter is still able to obtain the products, which she may need to survive. And in these days when so many corporations are interconnected, and so many multinationals are involved in unacceptable activity, shoplifting is a generalized protest: it is a refusal to put any cash into the economy at all, so the shoplifter can be sure that none of her cash will ever end up in the hands of the corporations she disapproves of. In addition to that, she will have to work less for them, as well!

But what about the people in the corporations? What about their welfare? First of all, corporations are distinct from traditional private businesses in that they exist as separate financial entities from their owners. So the shoplifter is stealing from a non-human entity, not directly from the pocket of a human being. Second, since so many workers are paid set wages (minimum wage, for example) that depend more on how little the corporation can get away with paying rather than on how much profit it is making, the shoplifter is not really hurting most of the workforce at any given company either. The stockholders, who are almost always far richer than your average thief, are the ones who stand to lose a little if the company suffers significant losses; but realistically, no campaign of shoplifting could be intense enough to force any of the wealthy individuals who profit from these companies into poverty. Besides, modern corporations have money set aside for shoplifting losses, because they anticipate them. That's correct—these corporations are aware that there is enough dissatisfaction with them and their capitalist economy that people are going to steal from them remorselessly. In that sense, shoplifters are just playing their role in society, just like C.E.O.s. More significantly, these corporations are cynical enough to go about their business as usual, even though they know this leaves many of their customers (and employees!) ready to steal anything from them that they can. If

they are willing to continue doing business in this way even when they are aware how many people it alienates, they should not be surprised that people continue stealing from them.

And as for the myth that shoplifting drives prices up for consumers: you don't think the prices you're paying are actually determined just by the costs of making and distributing the products, do you? Again, these corporations are charging you as much as they think they can get away with. The market, not their expenses, determines the prices. If the money they set aside for shoplifting losses doesn't get used, the owners are more likely to keep it for themselves or invest it in opening more shops (and thus running more independent businesses out of the market) than to share any of it with their much poorer employees, let alone pass it along to the consumer in decreased prices. If enough products were shoplifted from a corporate store that they had to raise their prices, that would drive customers out of their clutches and into less globally harmful local shops, anyway—does that sound so bad?

Shoplifting is more than a way to survive in the cutthroat competition of the "free market" and protest corporate injustices. It is also a different orientation to the world and life in general.

The shoplifter makes do with an environment that has been conquered by capitalism and industry, where everything has become private property and there is no longer a natural world from which to gather resources, without accepting it or the absurd way of life it entails. She takes her life into her own hands by applying an ancient method to the problem of modern survival: she lives by urban hunting and gathering. In this way she is able to live much as her distant ancestors did before the world was subjugated by technology, imperialism, and the irrational demands of the "free" market; and she can find the same challenges and rewards in her work, rewards that are lost to the rest of us today. For her, the world is as dangerous and as exciting as it was to prehistoric humanity: every day she is in new situations, confronting new risks, living by her wits in a constantly changing environment. For the law-abiding consumer, chances are that every day at work is similar to the last one, and danger is as sorely lacking in life as meaning and purpose are.

To shoplift is to affirm immediate, bodily desires (such as hunger) over abstract "ethics" and other such ethereal constructs, most of which are left over from a deceased Christianity anyway. Shoplifting divests the commodity (and the marketplace in general) of the mythical power it seems to have to control the lives of consumers . . . when

commodities are seized by force, they show themselves for what they are: merely resources that have been held by force by these corporations at the expense of everyone else. Shoplifting places us back in the physical world, where things are real, where things are nothing more than their physical characteristics (weight, taste, ease of acquisition) and are not invested with superstitious qualities such as "market value" and "profit margin." It forces us to take risks and experience life firsthand again. Perhaps shoplifting alone will not be able to overthrow industrial society or the capitalist system . . . but in the meantime it is one of the best forms of protest and self-empowerment, and one of the most practical, too!

THE STOCKHOLM ACTION

n grotesque, witless imitation of Swedish state employee unions, which have days on which extra workers volunteer for free to show how much better they could do their work if they had more funding, the Stockholm police announced that they too would have a "Safe Stockholm" day. On this day the entire police force, both on-duty and off-duty officers, was to man the streets of the city, the ostensible purpose being to demonstrate that adding even more police surveillance could somehow make the city a safer, more pleasant place.

A special meeting of the Swedish CrimethInc. team was called, and costume shops across the country were raided to outfit almost two hundred more "freelance police" for the occasion. These CrimethInc. police showed up in Stockholm that day alongside the official pigs, giving out tickets for absurd violations to passers by and caricaturing the usual offensiveness of police officers. They helped add to the frustration that average citizens felt about being surrounded by even more police than usual, and this frustration dispelled whatever festive atmosphere the event would have had for the pigs otherwise.

Around sundown, the police realized that some of their number were not only off-duty but counterfeit. They feared to arrest the troublemakers, since that might call into question the legality of having "freelance police" at all, but began to threaten and intimidate the CrimethInc. officers. This tactic failed, and their rage increased until one of the mock-cops attempted to perform a citizen's arrest upon a police sergeant in violation of a traffic code. At this provocation, a police riot broke out, the police rabidly assaulting the impostor police with billy clubs; but the CrimethInc. agents melted into the body of police around them, and soon no one could tell one side from the other. Furious and desperate to punish their enemies for humiliating them, the police attacked each other blindly, using tear gas and finally bullets. In all, thirty seven police officers and six CrimethInc. agents were injured.

A judge ruled that having off-duty police on patrol was illegal, and let the CrimethInc. agents go free while sternly reprimanding the police force, which was wracked by internal disorder in the wake of this catastrophe. And, bowing to public pressure, the government cut funding to the police department severely, rather than raising it as they had hoped.❀

☞*GRUNGE HITS SEATTLE, TURN TO PAGE 257*

is for Working

"Work is the very opposite of creation, which is play.

"The world only began to get something of value from me the moment I stopped being a serious member of society and became—*myself*. The State, the nation, the united nations of the world, were nothing but one great aggregation of individuals who repeated the mistakes of their forefathers. They were caught in the wheel from birth and they kept at it until death— and this treadmill they tried to dignify by calling it "life." If you asked anyone to explain or define life, what was the be-all and end-all, you got a blank look for an answer. Life was something which philosophers dealt with in books that no one read. Those in the thick of life, "the plugs in harness," had no time for such idle questions. *"You've got to eat, haven't you?"* This query, which was supposed to be a stopgap, and which had already been answered, if not in the absolute negative at least in a disturbingly relative negative by those who knew, was a clue to all the questions which followed in a veritable Euclidean suite. From the little reading I had done I had observed that the men who were most *in* life, who were molding life, who were life itself, ate little, slept little, owned little or nothing. They had no illusions about duty, or the perpetuation of their kith and kin, or the preservation of the State. They were interested in truth and in truth alone. They recognized only one kind of activity—*creation*. Nobody could command their services because they had of their own pledged themselves to give all. They gave gratuitously, because that is the only way to give. This was the way of life which appealed to me: it made sound sense. It *was* life—not the simulacrum which those about me worshipped."

–*Henry Miller*, The Revolution of Everyday Life

Tricks of the Tradeless

<u>Gregarius:</u> There are a thousand reasons not to work—to enjoy life more, to avoid the humiliation of putting a price on your time or wearing a uniform or having a boss, to deny the capitalist market your labor. And when I say "not work," I don't mean doing nothing instead, I mean having your time to spend on what you want to do. I think one of the best reasons to not work is the fact that so many people can't imagine what to do instead. You have to have the chance to reclaim your ability to direct your own energy. I wouldn't be able to do so much activist work, or travel so much, if I had a normal job— that's for sure.

Deborah: For me it's also about being as far out of the production-consumption circuit as I can be. If I have no money coming in, I'm not tempted to spend it on useless products . . . which first of all would keep me needing an income, stuck with only one lifestyle option—you can get so caught up in paying off the debts for the last stuff you bought to cheer you up, buying more stuff to fend off the anxiety about that, and so on—and second of all, it's ecologically right on too, not to encourage them to keep mass-producing shit when the landfills are already filled.

Paul: In my case, it was really tough at first, I'll admit—really awful for the first couple years, after I promised myself I'd never get another job, because I barely knew anyone else who was doing the same thing or had any knowledge to share with me. I practically had to learn it all on my own, which seems really sad now that I know how many other people there are doing similar things who could have helped me through the adjustment. All my old friends from college literally couldn't grasp the concept—they had all gotten jobs, or were getting money from their parents, and they'd complain like everyone does about money while they drank at a bar with a cover price or some other place I just couldn't afford to go; eventually we stopped seeing each other, simply because I couldn't afford it. There was a miserable period where I spent a lot of time by myself, wandering around, desperately looking for the necessities of existence. But I used the new time I had to get involved in projects that brought me into contact with new circles of friends, people who understood much better what I was doing and why. They've been able to help me a lot, and life is much better, now. Every day I wake up healthy and alive, every time I put food in my mouth without compromising myself for it, it's another little victory, another little proof to me that resistance really is possible.

Jay: It's different for me than for Paul, because I grew up really poor, I never had anything in the first place, including job options. For me, not working is just an extension of what I learned from growing up with my father unemployed, and then having to run away and live on the street . . . but doing it deliberately means I can make it a positive thing, and not feel like I'm hopelessly at the mercy of the economy. I could sit around being miserable, waiting for the chance to work every once in a while for some fast food shit, or I could do this. Really, since I've got nothing, I at least want to live my life to the fullest, to do the creative things I love.

<u>Markatos:</u> I worked full time originally, construction work, and then I started cutting back hours so I could have more time to work on my art . . . when I lost my job, I started just working at little jobs, setting up gallery exhibitions for commercial artists, catering, maybe a temporary two or three week blast of hard labor to pay for a couple months of freedom. I would get jobs because I wanted to learn something that they could teach me, like welding—not unlike the way Sarah gets a job at a copy shop for a week every time she finishes a new issue of her 'zine, just to rip off the copies. I found a really cheap house out here in the country, and planted a garden. At this point I only have to work a few weeks a year.

<u>Deborah:</u> If you want to do it, it's really just a question of jumping off the cliff: quit your job and don't look back—you're bound to land somewhere. I don't know anyone who hasn't eventually succeeded when they set out to make it work, once they believed they really could do it. There's not much in this world that can actually kill you. All that grey area that looks like death and disaster from the perspective of bourgeois security is a lot easier to deal with once you get up close to it.

<u>Gregarius:</u> If you're not ready to go the jobless route all out, like someone like Paul or Debbie, there are plenty of other options. I discovered juggling early on, and then I figured out that if I present myself right to the running dogs of corporate America they'll pay me $500 or more for single engagements. I made up fancy business cards, got myself an agent, and I'll perform perhaps twenty nights a year at their meetings and conventions. It's like highway robbery, basically, because it finances the rest of my life, which I use to undermine all their work. And there are other, less rare opportunities—if I wasn't doing this, I could get a paid position working for one of the activist groups I volunteer with. My friend Anna up here is manager of a non-profit radical bookstore, and that salary is enough for her to help out some of her less fortunate friends. That's an important part of this whole workless undertaking, to be able to recognize when you have more resources than other people and be willing to share them. I'm not saying you have to take care of everyone, but recognize that people might have something else to offer besides money, and don't be afraid to share with them what you have . . . like one of the guys who stays with her a lot does all the folding and stapling and other volunteer work for their newsletter, because he has the time and no one else does. When everyone is committed to giving their all to each other, it's wonderful to

be able to stop measuring, stop worrying about fair trade and equal exchanges and just give and share with people.

Jay: For a few years I was just hitchhiking, begging for change, hanging out with other homeless people . . . I had to fight pretty hard with depression, yeah. But I did other things, too, I always kept myself sharp in some way or another. Like when I was sleeping in the libraries, I taught myself to use their computers so I can program webpages and shit for my friends and for things we do . . . anyway, I got really lucky last year when I met Liz totally by accident on Lee Street. She's a professional writer, really cool even though she's completely middle class—I actually knew her daughters already. She has an overload of writing assignments— she's supposed to do all this boring shit for in-flight airplane magazines—so when she found out I can write too, she started having me do some of the assignments and letting me have the money. Now I'm the only one here with a decent income, even among my friends who came from  the middle class! It's weird. I guess the world will always surprise you, if you stay around long enough for it to.

Paul: I spend a lot of my time in the library on the college campus here—libraries are awesome, that's the way all property should be arranged anyway, and at this one I can get free books, movie showings, videos (they even have VCR's and TV's for us to use), access to the internet on computers, quiet rooms to sleep, bathrooms . . . and I can tape all the records I want when I sneak into the college radio station next door. I just try to be aware of all the stuff I can collect easily through urban hunting and gathering—toilet paper, matches, plates and silverware at corporate restaurants, free cassettes from record store giveaways—there's so much shit that goes to waste in the U.S., it's ridiculous. You can get almost anything out of a garbage can—food, furniture, I remember when Jay even found a fucking good guitar amplifier, that worked! You can also help out small businesses in return for their extras—I used to steal big cans of olives from the back room of the private dormitory cafeteria (it was open through the back door) and trade them for burritos at a little closet place—and then there's shoplifting, or getting free stuff from disgruntled employees, which is easy with so many people unhappy at their jobs . . . you should never pay for photocopies, or bagels, for example. Once I traded a few records to a friend for a good bicycle that had been abandoned at the bike repair shop where he worked! Then there are scams—once you know other people living the same lifestyle, a new one will come around every month or so: free phone calls, or postage stamps, or subway passes from some kind of trick. I've heard of some great ones, like in Abbie Hoffman's *Steal This Book* where he figures out which foreign coins can replace quarters perfectly in machines, and finds a struggling third world currency where he can trade twenty five cents for something like one hundred coins that can act as a quarter each! Learning to adapt yourself to living with fewer clothes and amenities is important, but that can be an empowering experience, too, it doesn't have to be humiliating the way it looks from a distance to an unreconstructed middle class kid. Oh yeah! It really helps save money and enables you to do more interesting stuff if you don't smoke, drink, or use drugs.

<u>Jackson:</u> I got lucky, I just did things I liked to do and my present source of income just fell into my lap. I was really into rare old comics and stuff like that, something none of my friends could understand, and I discovered I could make a fortune bootlegging. It's not a bad thing to do—the people who want this stuff have the money for it, and they wouldn't be able to get it otherwise, right? And it's a lot safer than the shit some of my career criminal friends do, like stealing cars. I live pretty comfortably—really, without people like me to support them, some of my more diehard anti-work friends would have a much harder time of it. I understand it's not so revolutionary to be a criminal—or an artist or entertainer, for that matter, like some of the other people you're interviewing—but seriously, everything is a compromise in this world, until we can get the whole thing changed around. It's

just a question of what you think the most effective compromise will be. And doing this, I get to have plenty of time and even extra money to dedicate to better things. Another thing I wanted to say—this lifestyle has really given me a different relationship to my fellow men. When you're working, and there's all that tension and competitiveness and hatred, it's so easy to be elitist and hostile. But now I automatically try to be nice to people, to figure out what we have to offer each other, and it's easier to get along with people because I don't feel threatened by them . . . except for the pigs, of course.

<u>Deborah:</u> If you live in places where squatting is an option, like New York or Europe, that's obviously the best way to get housing. There you're not paying rent, you're using space that is otherwise going to industrial waste—it's like dumpstering a home!—and you're putting your energy into building a space that is open to everyone, not another suburban sanctuary-prison. Other than that . . . my friend Mo lived in her truck for a couple years, and at one point Sarah was sleeping there during the day too, when she worked night shift at the copy store. It can be hard to keep up with your belongings, but it reminds you not to have too many and to always share and lend them out. The key with all of this is just to be innovative . . . like if you have nowhere else to stay, organize a camp-out protest on a college campus or something, and just stay there—be sure to tell the media how much you miss your home and pets and TV!

<u>Paul:</u> The bottom line to not working is that you are leaving your place in the every-man-for-himself economy behind, so you have to learn to work with others. Find a group of people and figure out what everyone has to contribute—it doesn't have to be anything material, necessarily, but you have to pledge to take care of each other. This applies to where you live most of all. When I was on my own at the beginning, I rented the most awful little rooms, at more money than I could possibly afford, and then I started living in storage spaces, sleeping in libraries, or worse arrangements. I've spent a couple years of my life just traveling across the world from one friend's house to another so I wouldn't have to pay rent, and that's OK, but you're still depending on other people to pay. The best thing is to get a group together and form a community space, one that is designed for practical purposes—not just to recover from school or work, like most housing—a warehouse space, or a big old house with a basement and an absentee landlord. You can use the space for great things, live really cheaply, learn how to share together . . . and you can pay all or part of the rent

with projects like shows, money from bands that practice or live there, things like that. It's just like being in a band and getting a van to share instead of all having individual cars. And living together you don't just share the weight of the struggle to survive, but you also learn how to get along and do things collectively, which is the most important thing of all.

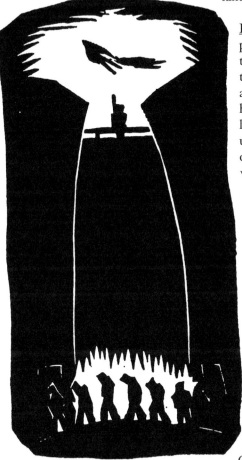

Elise: I don't know what other people can do for a place to live, there are probably a million options . . . what I did, I took over an abandoned shed behind a house where some kids I knew lived; it had only one wall, and using scraps of material from construction sites I rebuilt the whole thing and made it into a nice little house with a wood stove and everything. I even ran a phone cord out there from their house, started a garden, made my own fertilizer for it out of my own shit. I started the year with no idea how to do any of that stuff, except what I'd learned from working for a little while on an organic farm—it was incredible to find out I could do it all myself.

Jay: The hardest thing, of course, is getting medical care, but outside of places like Canada and northern European countries that still have a good social health care system, that's a problem for a lot of people who work all the time too. But you can usually figure it out somehow. I have one friend, god knows how many times he's been sick or hurt or infected on tour, and he always manages to find someone who can take care of him—some friend's mother is a doctor, or somebody is studying in nursing school, and then there's this one friend of theirs Sally who will go with them, and she's into all kinds of voodoo and older traditions of healing, she's really cool. There was Dan, I heard he faked an accident at his job to trick them into paying for surgery he needed when he had a slipped disc in his back— I think he got the job just to do that, that was some tough fucking shit. And Ernie just leaves his hospital bills unpaid, like I have before, like Cheese did when he got his jaw broken. He went there with his broken leg, then again with that abscess he had, and for some other shit, and got treatment every single time. It helps to keep moving around, to stay ahead of the bills . . . you can give a fake name, too. Stealing some vitamins and cooking that shit you get out of the dumpsters can be good preventative medicine, though—that's the best advice I can give.

Markatos: People ask me about what I want to do in the future, about having children, all that. As for a nice wife and fast-track career and fancy house and all that, I'm a grown man now and I find it hard to believe I'll have a reverse mid-life crisis and wish that I'd traded everything I've had for that bullshit. Honestly, even if I die tomorrow, I think the last ten years of adventure have been worth more to me than fifty years of any other life could be. I've had conflicts where I've been romantically involved with people who haven't been ready to go as far out as I am, but you can resolve those conflicts, it's not impossible—and I don't want to be involved with anyone who won't accept my way of life, that's ridiculous. As for kids, I think there are a lot of good reasons not to have children and right now I don't think I'll ever really want to. But I help my friends with their children, so I'm not excluding them from the possibility of enjoying this lifestyle. A couple good friends of mine are single mothers and I do what I can to babysit, bring them vegetables from our garden, that stuff. They're both awesome, still able to do a lot of great social work—although I'd like to mention that the welfare system in this country is totally fucked and provides no support for people like them, especially when they're trying to do good things for other people with their lives. But anyway, it'll be really interesting to see how those children grow up.

Elise: I certainly do want to have children one day. But when it comes to the issue of security and stability, I have no illusions that money and health insurance and all that stuff can provide more long-term security and safety than a real, loving community can. I think we either put our energies into surviving according to today's rules, or trying to make a world in which they are irrelevant. Someone's got to start to do that sometime. I know if I spend my life trying to build community with others, sharing what I have with them and doing things the way I feel is right, I'll have people there for me and my children when I need them. There are women's health clinics and places like that already that can provide support, they just need more people like me to devote our lives to them.

Paul: Sometimes people ask me if I feel like a parasite, living off the excess of this society. There's a lot I want to say about that. First, I know it's not possible for everyone in this country to do this—a lot of people have families to take care of, or want to try "working within the system," as they say, or are already coming from poverty—and that's OK. And more than that, a life like mine would be almost impossible in a place like Brazil where there are less resources to go around—they do have the M.S.T. that squats farmlands there, but that's not the same as the life I'm leading. Anyway—the fact that not everyone has the privilege to be able to arrange a work-free life for themselves is a good reason, in my opinion, why those of us who do have the chance should take it. I'm not tormented by any middle class guilt about the chances I have in my life, as long as I really use those chances to try to make chances available to other people too. I think those of us who have the privilege to take ourselves out of the system, the better to work for its downfall, have a responsibility to everyone else as well as ourselves to do just that, the more so because the poor factory worker father of three down the street and millions of people across the rest of the world don't have that option. Especially since there are so many things that go to waste in this society, why not put them to use, instead of helping to create more waste, more consumption? Don't people who participate in the status quo feel like parasites, destroying the earth and suppressing their own idealism in the process? No one is self-reliant, that's an American myth; the question is not whether you are paying your own way—everyone who has claimed to be doing that has always done it at the expense of others—but whether you are using whatever chances you have to make the world a better place. People have asked me before what would happen if more people would live the way I do, if the resources wouldn't run out. First of all, like I said before, the more people who are living like this the easier it is to do—so I think if more people join us outside the work system it can only help. And second of all—let's say that happens and the excess we've been living off of does run out—that will be a good thing, too. If you have a large number of people who are not willing to work inside the world of competition and corporate control anymore, who want more out of life than it has to offer and are sworn to never go back, and they can no longer get the resources they need to survive by collecting the leavings of the capitalist market . . . well, right there you have a revolutionary group that is totally ready to go. If the resolve and ambition of their desires could be infectious, so that others would join them in demanding back the resources of our society, that would quickly become "a situation that goes beyond the point of no return," in the words of the poets.

Gregarius: I know I can do this as long as I choose to. I've been lucky enough to find out how many different things are possible in life, things that I never could have seen from a more standard vantage point, and I've met so many other great people who are doing wild things with their lives, people who I know would help me or point me in new directions if I ever needed it. I believe in myself enough now enough that I'll be ready to try out whatever crazy plan I have next, no looking back. And I would absolutely recommend doing absurd things like quitting your job forever to anyone who wants to have a full, adventurous life.

OUT OF THE WAITING GAME AND INTO THE FIRE

The meeting of the World Trade Organization in Seattle was shut down by the intervention of over 20,000 civilians, and shortly thereafter the meeting of the I.M.F./World Bank in Washington, D.C. was similarly sabotaged. Thanks to the courage and cooperation of a variety of individuals and groups acting (consciously or not) according to the guidelines set forth in the CrimethInc. pamphlet *How to Throw a Proper Street Party,* people on the West and then East coasts of the U.S.A. discovered the joys of acting directly to achieve their goals instead of politely waiting for politicians and businessmen to consider their requests. In the process they happened upon a perfect integration of the methods and desires of all who were present at the demonstrations, from well-be-

haved sign-holders to black-masked corporate-window-display-smashing anarchists. Some of the "peaceful" protesters misunderstood how much more seriously their demands were taken thanks to the threat implied by the direct actions of the more radical participants, but the lesson was not wasted on posterity.

YOU FIND THE NEAREST WEAPON, GO OUT TO THE STREETS, AND START YOUR OWN . . .

PRESENT CRIMETHINC. PROJECTS

Ongoing CrimethInc. activities as of this writing include several publications (magazines and tabloids covering a variety of subjects, one local newspaper, and a whole host of independently published "'zines"), writers' groups, hiking and camping clubs, urban hunter/gatherer teams, political action cells (involved in projects ranging from Reclaim the Streets, Food Not Bombs, and Critical Mass to more clandestine undertakings), squats and community centers, free stores and cafés, book and literature distributors, graffiti and postering teams, thieves' guilds, and experimental art/music collectives . . . as well as several less specific projects and a few we would do well not to mention. The following pages offer a few examples of posters used in postering campaigns over the past year.

An Incomplete List of CrimethInc. Departments

CrimethInc. Anti-Ennui Strike Force
CrimethInc. Action Faction
CrimethInc. Bureau of Investigations
CrimethInc. Conspiracy Theorists
CrimethInc. Dance Troops
    (aka Shock Troupes)
CrimethInc. Eastern Writers' Bloc
CrimethInc. Inner Circle
CrimethInc. Joy Division
CrimethInc. Revolutionary Cells
CrimethInc. Revolutionary Dance Party
CrimethInc. Society of Secret Celebrities
CrimethInc. Special Forces
CrimethInc. ThInc. Tank
CrimethInc. Vanguard of the Sexual
    Revolution
CrimethInc. Vice Squad
CrimethInc. Witness Protection Program
CrimethInc. Worker Collective
    (aka Ex-Workers' Collective)

Abaddon Graphics Team
A.T.R. Group
Black Bloc, The
Experamen
Fifth Column Conspiracy
F.B.I. Insurgency Group
F.C.
No Surrender Cell
Paper Street Bandits
Paul F. Maul Artists' Group
Personal Autonomy Cells
Ten Millimeter Gang
Terminal Lead Works
Train Bridge Recluse Publishing
Weather Underground
White African Fags

We categorically deny all rumors that there is or ever has been a division of CrimethInc. that functions as a record label. To permit such an inherently capitalist project to take place under the auspices of our revolutionary program would be absurdly hypocritical. And in case it should ever happen that someone finds evidence proving such a thing exists, we declare in advance that the involved parties have all been expelled from the collective and their department declared apocryphal. ☞ *WHAT HAPPENS NEXT IS UP TO YOU!*

you will find
your only
safety
is in
danger

CrimethInc.

Would you like to pay by personal check, or credit card? Money order, cash up front, put it on lay-away, financing and no money down? Automatic withdrawals to pay off the bank loans, college loans, Visa and Mastercard debts, State and Federal taxes, rent and food and health "care," a thousand banalities that keep you running like a hamster in a wheel between the classroom and the sucky job and the marriage altar, the freeway and the office and the corporate golf course meeting? Death on the installment plan, or all at once like a stockbroker mid-life crisis suicide on the next Black Monday?

Or would you really like something else, something altogether different? Would you like not to pay at all, never to pay again for land and food and even water? 100% off, everything MUST go! Have you ever had a dream in which everything was free, and you could eat whatever you wanted and go wherever you wanted and do anything you wanted? Have you ever wanted to have enough of everything that you could share freely with everyone else, without worrying about spending your resources "efficiently" and "responsibly"? Ever wanted to quit being responsible for one moment and just do what your heart demands?

What "insurance" could you buy that would keep you safer than living in a world where people actually cared about each other?

Perhaps you should find yourself some like-minded friends, stop talking about how bad traffic was and start discussing *tactics.* Or swear to yourself that you will never, ever again do anything but chase your wildest dreams, every moment of your life. Or buy yourself a liter of gasoline and a bottle. It could be your last purchase ever.

Anarchy.

**Once you've tried it,
nothing else compares.**

**you have to realize that
someday you will die.
until you know that,
you are useless.**

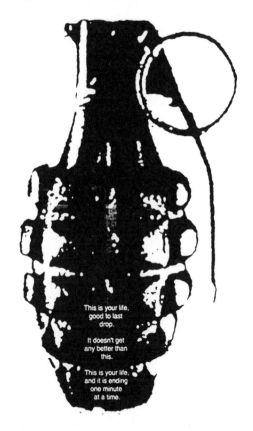

This is your life,
good to last
drop.

It doesn't get
any better than
this.

This is your life,
and it is ending
one minute
at a time.

**it is only after you have lost
everything that you are free
to do anything**

THE TEN MILLIMETER GANG
a Personal Autonomy List

crimethinc.

there is no need for us to invent anything
you already know what we mean
we are already inside your head
you can already read it
you can already feel it within yourself

this begins with you YOU

we all know it's wrong but we
don't speak up. we don't speak up. I'm unsure and
I'm afraid and I don't really know if this is the
right thing to do. But I tell you this:
the silence ends here and now.

THE ONES WHO STRIKE THE BLOWS FORGET

THE ONES WHO BEAR
THE SCARS

REMEMBER

What's the price on your head?
dishwasher $6.00/hour,
grill cook $6.50/hour,
prostitute $60-200/hour . . .

a new reality is better than a new movie

a fantasy of defeat,

an escape into chains,

a vacation at a dead end

I REALISED THEN — IF YOU WANT SOMETHING DONE THEN YOU'VE GOT TO DO IT YOURSELF — DIRECT ACTION IS THE ANSWER —

life can be beautiful when we start to

break free!

hedonism.

ambitious hedonism.

Be like **Ted**

Just undo it.

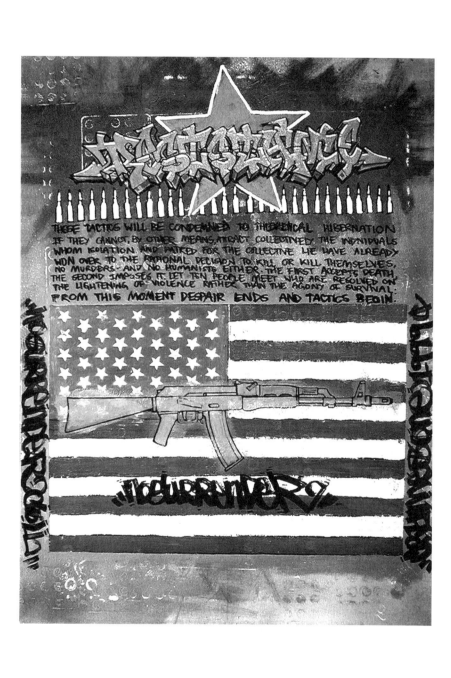

THESE TACTICS WILL BE CONDEMNED TO THEORETICAL HIBERNATION IF THEY CANNOT, BY OTHER MEANS, ATTRACT COLLECTIVELY THE INDIVIDUALS WHOM ISOLATION AND HATRED FOR THE COLLECTIVE WE HAVE ALREADY WON OVER TO THE RATIONAL DECISION TO KILL OR KILL THEMSELVES. NO MURDERS AND NO HUMANISTS EITHER. THE FIRST ACCEPTS DEATH. THE SECOND IMPOSES IT. LET TEN PEOPLE MEET WHO ARE RESOLVED ON THE LIGHTENING OF VIOLENCE RATHER THAN THE AGONY OF SURVIVAL. FROM THIS MOMENT DESPAIR ENDS AND TACTICS BEGIN.

$$\frac{x}{\infty} = \text{your life}$$

Conclusion:

Out of This World

"Where do you want to go, my heart?"
"Anywhere—anywhere, out of this world."

Afterworld by Gloria Cubana

Whatever medical science may profess, there is a difference between Life and survival. There is more to being alive than just having a heartbeat and brain activity. Being *alive,* really alive, is something much subtler and more magnificent. Their instruments measure blood pressure and temperature, but overlook joy, wonder, love, all the things that make life really matter. To make our lives matter again, to really get the most out of them, we will have to redefine life itself. We have to dispense with their merely clinical definitions, in favor of ones which have more to do with what we actually feel.

As it stands, how much *living* do you have in your life? How many mornings do you wake up feeling truly free, thrilled to be alive, breathlessly anticipating the experiences of a new day? How many nights do you fall asleep feeling fulfilled, going over the events of the past day with satisfaction? Many of us feel as though everything has already been decided without us, as if living is not a creative activity but rather something that happens *to* us. That's not being *alive,* that's just surviving: being undead. We have undertakers, but their services are not usually required; we have morgues, but we spend most of our time in office cubicles and video arcades, in shopping malls, in front of televisions. Of course suburban housewives and petty executives are terrified of risk and change; they can't imagine that there is anything more valuable than physical safety. Their hearts may be beating, but they no longer believe in their dreams, let alone chase after them.

But this is how the revolution begins: a few of us start chasing our dreams, breaking our old patterns, embracing what we love (and in the process discovering what we hate), daydreaming, questioning, acting outside the boundaries of routine and regularity. Others see us doing this, see people daring to be more creative and more adventurous, more generous and more ambitious than they had imagined possible, and join us one by one. Once enough people embrace this new way of living, a point of critical mass is finally reached, and society itself begins to change. From that moment, the world will start to undergo a transformation: from the frightening, alien place that it is, into a place ripe with possibility, where our lives are in our own hands and any dream can come true.

So do what you want with your life, whatever it is! But to be sure you do get what you want, think carefully about what it really is, first, and how to go about getting it. Analyze the world around you, so you'll know which people and forces are working against your desires, and which ones are on your side . . . and how you can work together with us. We're out here, living life to the fullest, waiting for you— hopping trains across the United States, organizing demonstrations in the streets of London, writing beautiful letters at sunrise in Bangkok. We just finished making love in the corporate washroom a minute before you walked in on your half hour lunchbreak.

And Life is waiting for you with us, on the peaks of unclimbed mountains, in the smoke of campfires and burning buildings, in the arms of lovers who will turn your world upside down. Come join us!

Paul— never got around to doing the bibliography — here are all the ~~names~~ books and films and etc. we voted on, please type up a full reference for each one — thanks...

—BOOKS— F. Block's Weetzie Bat

George Orwell — 1984, Homage to Catalonia

J.D. Salinger —— The Inverted Forest

our own Jeanette Winterson —
- the Passion
- Sexing the Cherry
- Written on the Body
- The World and other Places

Henry Miller: Sexus, Tropics of Cancer and Capricorn...

Herman Hesse — Demian, Steppenwolf, Beneath the Wheel

Sartre: Nausea

Guy Debord — Society of the Spectacle (and all that other Situ. stuff)

Raoul Vaneigem — Revolution of Everyday Life

that Autonomedia book "Cracking the Movement"

Marshall MacLuhan's "The Medium = the message"

Grendel!

Albert Camus — the Fall, a Happy Death

what's-his-name: Catch 22

Abbie Hoffman — Steal this Book, Revolution for the Hell of it

Jerry Rubin — Do It!

Aldous Huxley's Brave New World

Clifford Harper's "Anarchy: A Graphic Guide"

Moby Dick!

Evening, by what's-her-name

The Painted Bird, On the Road,

Burroughs' Naked Lunch, Marquez's 100 Years of Solitude, The Unbearable Lightness of Being...

—MOVIES—

Natural Born Killers
Thin Red Line
Apocalypse Now
The Seventh Seal
Before the Revolution
The English Patient (or maybe this should go w/ books)
Fight Club
The Pillow Book
Pleasantville
Dead Man
Metropolis
Cinema Paradiso

—POETRY—

That great book "The Hand that Cradles the Rock..."

Elliot's Waste Land

—PLAYS—

Peter Schaffer's Equus and Royal Hunt of the Sun

—ARTISTS—

Ernst Fuchs, Kathe Kollwitz, Egon Schiele, Edvard Munch, Kubin, Böcklin, Klinger...

—♫—

Godspeed, You Black Emperor!
Diamanda Galàs
Magnetic Fields
last REFUSED LP
His Hero Is Gone

INDEX

About the Authors

Nadia C. is a freelance wrioter and dilettante romantic of Eastern European dissent. The rest is secrets.

Gloria Cubana is an itinerant lover and clandestine poet raised in the American South. She's presently hard at work on her second book, *The Unauthorized Autobiography of Gloria Cubana*. She has also published a series of atlases and a travel guide entitled *The Moon on $47 Million a Day*.

Frederick Markatos Dixon, Eagle Scout, folk scientist, detective, keen intuition, intense love for peanut butter, maker of working infrasonic weapon, owner of two sets of clothes, four hundred pounds of tools, six US patents and one cat, retired from Arkansas kitty litter mine in 1992, lives in a shotgun shack on a Christmas tree farm, central North Carolina.

NietzsChe Guevara is a professor of philosophy and Latin American guerrilla warrior. His published works include *Lifestyle Monarchism, or Anarcheology!* and *Plato Will Kill Us All*.

Jane E. Humble is a recently graduated sorority sister from the American heartland. In addition to caring for her daughters and authoring children's books, she enjoys cooking, knitting, and grossly deviant sexual practices.

Paul F. Maul is a former teenage heartthrob, self-taught graphic artist, and car thief turned terrorist and assassin. Expect to hear more about him soon.

Stella Nera, renowned feminista freedom fighter and student of Sufi mysticism, is now years into a worldwide dérive.

Tristran Tzarathustra grew up in Zurich, Switzerland, in the same building that Lenin lived in during the first world war— about fifty paces from the Cabaret Voltaire at which Lenin was known to spend his time with the Dada anti-artists. Tristran is best known for his inflammatory work *Do What Must Be Done*.

Jeanette Winterson is a widely acclaimed British novelist and critic.

The general has only eighty men, and the enemy five thousand. In his tent the general curses and weeps. Then he writes an inspired proclamation and homing pigeons shower copies over the enemy camp. Two hundred desert on foot to the general. There follows a skirmish which the general wins easily, and two regiments come over to his side. Three days later, the enemy has only eighty men and the general five thousand. The general writes another proclamation and seventy-nine more men join up with him. Only one enemy is left, surrounded by the army of the general, who waits in silence. The night passes and the enemy has not come over to his side. The general curses and weeps in his tent. At dawn the enemy slowly unsheathes his sword and advances on the general's tent. He goes in and looks at him. The army of the general disbands. The sun rises.

WANTED:

Creative, independent men and women, tired of being exhausted by the trivial details of modern survival, fed up with the misery of modern entertainment, no longer confused by the distractions of the mass media . . . not content with limiting their freedom, their lives, to their so-called "free time." People who prefer idealism to realism, and reality to ideology.

To become **full-time revolutionaries.** NOT armchair revolutionaries, not ivory tower revolutionaries, not weekend revolutionaries. And not "professional" revolutionaries, either: rather than making a business out of "revolution," they must *make revolution their business.* Men and women who will not allow their efforts to win back their freedom to become just another job, who are ready to live according to their desires *around the clock.*

Punk Rockers, Activists—don't be content to live in a world of your own making only once a week, when a band plays or a protest takes place. Demand that excitement every day, demand that self-determination every morning when you wake up. Ask yourself: do you want the *symbols* of rebellion, or rebellion itself?

Musicians, Artists—seek not to "make a living from your art," as any worker who sells his labor (and thus his creativity) for money does. Seek to make art your way of living—or, even better, *make living your art.* We must

an invitation

use our creativity not to make more *representations* of reality, but to transform reality itself. To concentrate our vast abilities on anything less would be to cheat ourselves of a world.

Life is contagious, you know: if you want to make others feel it, you must live it to the fullest yourself, so that it will call out to them through you. If you would make art to share with them, you must first share yourself, give yourself to life and passion . . .

Human Beings—Look at the world around us; it is a world that we have created. We transformed the old world into this one—but why *this* one? Is this the world we would have chosen, if we had considered in advance the question of what the best of all possible worlds might be? But before you despair, think—we created this world, it is we who make it up. Could we not make another world out of it, then, if we preferred?

JOIN US. We have chosen to live our lives for ourselves, to make each day an adventure rather than a ritual—to pursue our dreams at any cost. Perhaps we can transform the world around us, in the same way that we transform our own lives. But this transforming, too, must be an adventure . . . for our revolution is, itself, the very joy we take in it. Write and offer your life if you dare.

Active Resistence, Passionate Existence
CrimethInc. Headquarters
2695 Rangewood Dr.
Atlanta GA 30345
USA

crimethinc.com(munication)
hello@crimethinc.com

Visual cuisine prepared by the GutF*Mud Artists Group, all natural ingredients hand picked, diced, chopped, puréed, squeezed, baked, fried, sautéed and grilled by RatFink!, with help from A- and E-